NFT and Crypto Art

2021

The Ultimate Beginner's Guide. Use Non-Fungible Tokens to Build Digital Assets and Learn Proven Strategies to Buy, Sell and Invest in Collectible Artworks.

are owned by the owners themselves, not affiliated with this document.

Table of Contents

CHAPTER 1

Introduction

Art, music, game goods, and movies are all examples of digital assets that reflect real-world things such as NFTs. The majority of them are purchased and sold online, often in cryptocurrency exchange, and they are usually programmed using the same underlying software as many other digital currencies.

However, despite the fact that they have been available since 2014, NFTs are growing in popularity due to the statistic that they are becoming an increasingly popular method of purchasing and selling digital artwork. Since November 2017, a whopping $174 million has been spent on NFTs, which is an all-time high.

Aside from that, NFTs are usually unique, or at the very least one of a very limited run, and unique identification codes identify them. According to Arry Yu, head of the Washington Technology Industry Association Cascadia Blockchain Council and managing director of Yellow Umbrella Ventures, "in essence, NFTs generate digital scarcity."

This is in striking contrast to the vast majority of digital works, which are virtually always available in an unlimited quantity. Thus, if a specific item is in high demand, shutting down the supply of that asset should, increase the value of that asset.

In reality, many NFTs have been digital works that already exist in some form in other places, such as famous video clips from NBA games or securitized copies of digital art that is already floating around on Instagram, at least in their early stages.

A well-known digital artist, better known as "Beeple," created "EVERYDAYS: The First 5000 Days" from a composite of 5,000 daily drawings, which became the most expensive NFT ever sold at Christie's for a world record-breaking $69.3 million in 2011.

Online, anybody may see individual images—or even the whole collage of images—for no charge at any time. As a result, individuals are ready to pay millions of dollars on something that they could simply capture or download for free.

Because a non-financial transaction enables the buyer to retain ownership of the original object. Not only that, but it also has built-in authentication, which acts as a means of establishing evidence of ownership. It is nearly as valuable as the object itself to collectors for them to have those "digital bragging rights."

How Is an NFT Different from Cryptocurrency?

NFT is an abbreviation for non-fungible token. Generally speaking, it is created using the same kind of programming as cryptocurrencies, such as Bitcoin or Ethereum, but that is about where the similarities between them stop.

Currency in the form of physical money and cryptocurrencies are both "fungible," meaning they may be traded or swapped with one another. They're also the same in terms of value: one dollar is always worth another dollar, and one Bitcoin is always worth another Bitcoin, and so on. Because of crypto currency's fungibility, it is a reliable method of completing transactions on the blockchain.

NFTs, on the other hand, are unique. Each NFT is protected by a digital signature, which makes it impossible for them to be traded for or equated with one another in any way (hence, non-fungible). For example, one NBA Top Shot clip is not equivalent to EVERYDAYS just because they are both non-first-time attempts. It's worth noting that one NBA Top Shot footage is not always equivalent to another NBA Top Shot clip, however.

CHAPTER 2

The History of NFT

CryptoArt was inspired by cultural phenomena such as CryptoPunks, Rare Pepe, and CryptoKitties, which helped to establish the genre. These works of 'art' acquired popularity as a result of the viral network effects that accompanied them, as well as the urge to spend huge amounts of money to acquire them.

2012-2013: Colored Coins

Let's get started since this is a lengthy tale involving many individuals, artists, and projects, so let's get started.

It was via the use of a "colored coin," which was first released on the Bitcoin blockchain in 2012-2013, that the concept of NFTs was born. Colored coins are digital tokens that reflect real-world assets on the blockchain. According to the blockchain, they may be used to establish ownership of any item, from precious metals to automobiles to real estate, and even stocks and bonds. Although not as complex as the current concept, the initial concept utilized the Bitcoin blockchain to store assets such as digital collectibles, coupons, real estate, business shares, and other types of securities. They were referred to as "new technology" and "raw potential" for future use, and they were presented as such.

2014: Counterparty

Founded in 2014 on the Bitcoin blockchain, Counterparty is a peer-to-peer financial board and distributed, open-source internet protocol based on the blockchain technology. Counterparty enabled users to build their own tradable assets and to trade them on a decentralized exchange, allowing them to establish their own transferable currencies. In addition, it offered a plethora of ideas and possibilities, like meme trading without the concerns about counterfeiting.

Spells of Genesis on the Counterparty in 2015

Counterparty formed a partnership with the Spells of Genesis development team in April of this year. Using the Counterparty network, the Spells of Genesis game developers were not only among the first to issue in-game assets on the blockchain, but they were also among the first to conduct an initial coin offering (ICO). In addition, introducing their own in-game money, BitCrystals, the Counterparty developers were able to contribute to the game's development.

2016: Trading Cards on Counterparty

New fashion trends started to emerge in August of 2016. Earlier this year, Counterparty partnered with Force of Will, a well-known trading card game, to bring their cards to the Counterparty marketplace. According to sales volume, Force of Will was the fourth most popular card game in North America, behind only Pokemon, Yu-Gi-Oh!, and Magic. In spite of that they had no previous blockchain or cryptocurrency expertise, their entry into the ecosystem served as a testament to the need of placing such assets on a blockchain.

2016: Rare Pepes on Counterparty

Memes made their way onto the blockchain in 2016. Memes first appeared on the Counterparty platform in October of 2016, and have since spread across the community. People began to add assets to a specific meme dubbed "Rare Pepes," which was popular at the time. Rare Pepes are a meme that features an intriguing frog figure that has amassed a large and loyal following over the course of many years. What began as a humorous figure called Pepe the Frog has grown into one of the most famous memes on the internet, and is now considered a cultural phenomenon. Rare Pepes began to be exchanged on the Ethereum platform in early 2017, as the cryptocurrency gained in popularity. Portion's founder, Jason Rosenstein, worked with Louis Parker to organise the first live Rare Pepe auction, which took place during the first Rare Digital Art Festival in New York City in October. With the release of the Rare Pepe Wallet, CryptoArt was created, marking the first time that artists from all over the globe were able to submit and sell their own work. It was also the first time that digital art could be considered valuable in and of itself.

2017: Cryptopunks

As the trade of Rare Pepes became more popular, John Watkinson and Matt Hall, the founders of Larva Labs, developed unique characters that were produced on the Ethereum blockchain. There would be no two identical characters, and the total number of characters would be restricted to 10,000. The project's name, Cryptopunks, was inspired by a Bitcoin experiment conducted in the 1990s, and it may be characterized as a mix of the ERC721 and ERC20 protocols.

Even while ERC20, the most widely used Ethereum Token Standard, has rules that enable tokens to interact with one another, it is not the ideal choice for generating one-of-a-kind cryptographic tokens. Then there's ERC721, which was created with the goal of becoming the de facto standard for NFTs on the Ethereum blockchain. The ERC721 standard facilitates the monitoring of individual token ownership and movement from a single smart contract.

CryptoKitties NFTs got off to a flying start thanks to the ERC721. Using Ethereum, they operate as a virtual game built on the blockchain that enables users to adopt, breed, and exchange virtual cats with other players. They gained widespread attention and featured on various news broadcasts, including CNBC and Fox News. Axiom Zen, a Vancouver-based business, developed CryptoKitties, and rapidly gained popularity, resulting in the company receiving financing from prominent investors as a result of the increase in users. Dapper Labs was formed when Axiom Zen separated from CryptoKitties.

2018-2021: The NFT Explosion

Between 2018 and 2021, NFTs gradually gain public recognition before bursting into widespread acceptance in the first half of the year 2021.

The apparently clandestine trend that was sweeping the crypto-community by storm has been steadily migrating into more popular art forms over the last several years. This shift reached a tipping point on Valentine's Day 2018, when artist Kevin Abosch collaborated with GIFTO to hold a charity auction to benefit the organization. The collaboration resulted in a $1 million transaction, including a stunning piece of CryptoArt known as The Forever Rose.

With the use of the Ethereum blockchain in conjunction with his own blood in a project known as "IAMA Coin," Mr. Abosch proceeded to increase the stakes even more. Notably, Abosch is not the first artist to have experimented with this fascinating mode of expression. It has steadily gained popularity among artists who are eager to push the limits of their artistic expression.

The non-financial transaction market (NFT) is more efficient and more liquid than the traditional ways of moving assets. As a result, a slew of new platforms have sprung up on the internet, each offering something unique for both artists and collectors. The primary area of disruption is centered on reducing centralized costs, as conventional art brokers, auction houses, and other institutions typically take up to 40% of the sale price as their commission. Opensea is widely regarded as the world's biggest marketplace for fine art, music, domain names, collectibles, and trading cards, among other things. Mintable's platform is designed to make the minting process as simple as possible for the artists that use it. Portion is presenting itself as an NFT platform that connects NFTs, DeFi, and DAOs, with the power to make decisions resting with the holders of the governance token $PRT – the community — rather than the company. Other systems, like as Niftex, enable users to purchase fractions of NFTs, known as "shards," which are ERC20 tokens that represent a portion of a complete NFT in exchange for ERC20 tokens.

CHAPTER 3

The Basics of NFT

What are NFTs? Key terms explained

First and foremost, let's take a look at some of the important terminology and definitions that will be used throughout this course. In order to comprehend what NFTs are and how they function, we must first grasp some wider context:

NFT

NFT is an abbreviation for non-fungible token. That probably doesn't signify much at this point, since the term 'fungible' isn't one that is often used in everyday conversation. However, it basically implies that anything may be swapped out for another.

Money, for example, is considered a fungible asset in economics. In addition, it is divided into units that may be readily interchanged (for example, exchanging a £20 for two £10s) without affecting its worth. In addition to these items, fungible assets include things like gold, cryptocurrencies, and stocks.

As we learned in our cryptocurrency introduction phase, a fungible asset is something that can be divided up in a multiple ways and has an infinite number of them available. Therefore, in a variety of applications, such as payments and value storage, they may be utilized in many ways.

A non-fungible asset, on the other hand, is anything that exists just once; for example, a painting, a home, or a trading card. If you want to copy or photograph a painting, the original will always remain the original, and replicas will never have the same value as originals.

NFTs are data units that are kept on a blockchain, which is a digital ledger. Each non-fungible token serves as a sort of digital proof of authenticity, demonstrating that a digital asset is one-of-a-kind and cannot be exchanged for another. Furthermore, an NFT can never be altered, modified, and stolen due to the cryptographic principles that distinguish the blockchain from other digital ledgers.

Asset in the digital realm

Simply said, a digital asset is everything that exists in a digital format and that the owner of the asset has the right to utilize (a right to copy, duplicate, reproduce, modify and otherwise use). For example, digital assets include items such as papers, audio or video material, pictures, and other comparable digital data stored digitally.

Blockchain

This essay will supply you with an in-depth knowledge of blockchain technology, cryptocurrencies, and bitcoin. A blockchain is a kind of database, which means it is a collection of electronically recorded information or data. We examined this in more detail in our previous article.

A blockchain, as opposed to a traditional database, is a collection of data 'blocks' that are connected together. These blocks are linked together to establish a shared digital ledger (collection of data) that records the activities and information that occurs inside the network.

Each blockchain ledger is maintained on hundreds of different servers all over the world, allowing for worldwide access. This implies that everyone connected to the network may see (and verify) everyone else's entries. A block of data is virtually difficult to falsify or tamper with because of this peer-to-peer and distributed ledger technology, as it is often called.

According to IBM's definition, blockchain is a distributed, immutable (i.e., permanent and unalterable) ledger that makes the process of recording transactions and monitoring assets much more efficient and effective.

When we think about NFTs, we should remember that they are generated on a blockchain and cannot be transferred to another blockchain environment. However, it will live on that blockchain and prove the legitimacy of the item you have bought from them.

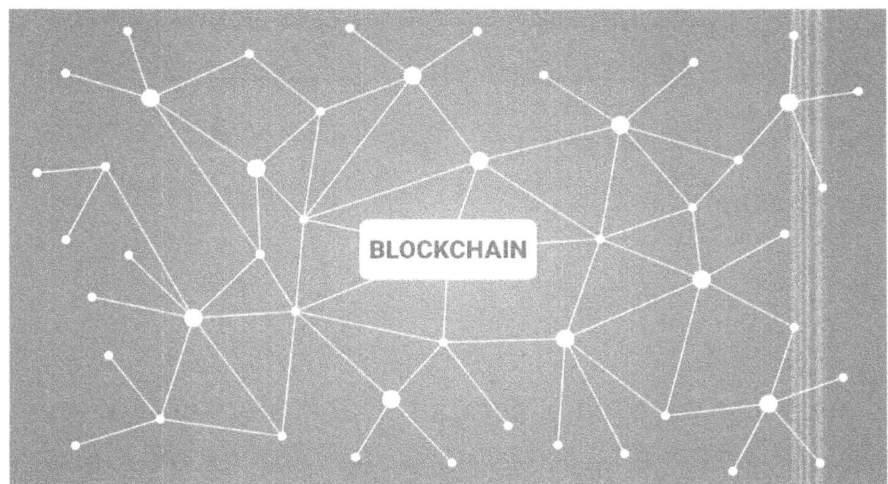

Who can create NFTs?

Creating an NFT is something anybody can do — from artists to businesspeople to art advocates to businesses to writers to videographers to social media celebrities to ordinary Joes and Joannas. There is no need for prior expertise, and as long as someone can demonstrate that they produced or legally own the material, they may mint an NFT.

How Does an NFT Work?

The blockchain, which is a distributed public register that records transactions, is where NFTs are stored. You're probably most acquainted with blockchain since it's the fundamental mechanism that enables cryptocurrencies like bitcoin and litecoin feasible.

In particular, NFTs are usually stored on the Ethereum blockchain, but they may be stored on other blockchains as well.

- Art
- GIFs
- Videos and sports highlights
- Collectibles
- Virtual avatars and video game skins
- Designer sneakers
- Music

Even tweets are taken into consideration. Jack Dorsey -Twitter co-founder- sold his first ever tweet as an NFT for more over $2.9 million, making him the richest person in the world.

In essence, NFTs are similar to real collector's goods, except that they are digital. As a result, the customer receives a digital copy rather than receiving a real oil painting to put on his or her wall.

In addition, they are granted exclusive ownership rights. That's correct: NFTs can only have a single owner at a given moment. Because each NFT has a unique ID, verifying ownership and transferring tokens between different owners is simple. The owner or author can keep particular information inside them. For example, using an NFT's metadata, artists may sign their work by adding their signature in the file's information.

What Are NFTs Used For?

Artists and content producers have a unique chance to monetize their work thanks to blockchain technology and non-fungible tokens (NFTs). When it comes to selling their artwork, artists no longer have to depend on galleries or auction houses. An NFT, on the other hand, may be sold directly to the customer by the artist and allows them to retain a larger portion of the earnings. Apart from that, artists have the option of programming royalties into their artwork so that they earn a portion of revenues every time their work is sold to a new owner. This is a desired feature since, in most cases, artists do not earn any further profits once their artwork has been sold.

Art Is not the only way to earn money with NFTs; there are other options as well. Brands such as Charmin and Taco Bell have auctioned off themed NFT paintings in order to generate money for charitable causes, among others. For example, "NFTP" (non-fungible toilet paper) was named by Charmin, and Taco Bell's NFT art sold out in minutes, with the top bids coming in at 1.5 wrapped ether (WETH), which is equivalent to $3,723.83 at the time of writing.

Nyan Cat, a GIF depicting a cat with a pop-tart body that was created in 2011, sold for almost $600,000 in February. In addition, as of late March, NBA Top Shot had earned more than $500 million in sales. A single LeBron James highlight NFT sold for more than $200,000 at an auction in New York.

A growing number of celebrities, like Snoop Dogg and Lindsay Lohan, are hopping on the NFT bandwagon and issuing securitized NFTs that include unique memories, artwork, and experiences.

How to Buy NFTs

If you wanna create your own NFT collection, you'll need to get your hands on a few crucial things, which are as follows:

First, it is essential to get a digital wallet that will enable you to store both NFTs and bitcoins. Depending on the currencies your NFT provider supports, you'll most likely need to buy some cryptocurrency, like as Ether, to get started. You may now purchase cryptocurrency using a credit card on sites such as Coinbase, Kraken, eToro, PayPal, and Robinhood, among others. After that, you will be capable to transfer it from the exchange to your preferred wallet of choice.

When researching your choices, bear in mind that there are costs to consider. For example, when you purchase cryptocurrency, the majority of exchanges charge you at least a portion of your transaction.

What makes NFTs so special?

Non-fungible tokens have unique attributes; they are usually linked to a specific asset. For example, they may be used to verify the ownership of digital goods like gaming skins and the ownership of real assets such as land and buildings.

Other tokens, like coins and banknotes, are fungible in the same manner as coins and banknotes are. Thus, when two fungible tokens are traded, they are similar in that they have the same characteristics and value.

What is the purpose of non-fungible tokens?

Non-fungible tokens may be used for a variety of digital assets, including crypto-collectibles such as CryptoKitties, as well as for digital assets that must be distinguished from one another in order to demonstrate their worth or scarcity. They may represent everything from virtual property parcels to artworks to ownership licenses, and anything in between besides.

In contrast to fungible tokens, which are exchanged on traditional cryptocurrency exchanges, non-fungible tokens are purchased and sold on digital markets such as Openbazaar or Decentraland's Land marketplace.

Non-fungible tokens vs cryptocurrency

It's critical to understand the difference between cryptocurrency and non-fungible tokens before proceeding. Despite the fact that both are built on blockchain technology, understanding the basic distinctions between the two may aid in our understanding of how NFTs operate.

The fundamental distinction stems from the fact that bitcoin is fungible. You may, for example, trade one Bitcoin for another Bitcoin if you want to. You cannot, however, do so in the case of an NFT. In contrast to fungible tokens, non-fungible tokens are linked to a specific digital asset and cannot be replaced.

What is the reason behind the value of NFTs?

For those who are unfamiliar with the term "non-fungible token," it refers to an asset that does not have a physical counterpart. Amounts owed to an asset are determined by the asset's collectibility as well as the asset's potential for resale. NFTs are available for purchase and trade.

Once again, the use of art serves as an excellent illustration of the importance of NFTs. During a Christie's auction in February 2021, digital artist Beeple sold the NFT from their Everydays – The First five thousand Days artwork for a whopping $69.3 million, setting a new record.

Examples of non-traditional sales

It is not just NFT art that is in high demand. There have been many noteworthy sales of NFTs in recent months, which has led some to speculate that the market is now experiencing a bubble at the present (more on that later).

The following are some instances of NFT sales:

- **The very first Twitter message**. With the sale of the NFT for his first Tweet, Twitter creator Jack Dorsey made $2.9 million dollars.

- **The animated gif of the 'Nyan Cat**.' The NFT for the vibrant GIF was sold for 300 Ether (a cryptocurrency), which was worth about $561,000 at the time of the sale.

- **The video titled "Charlie Bit Me**." Over 800 million people have seen the viral video of a baby chewing his brother's finger, which was uploaded on YouTube. The NFT used in the video was sold for about £500,000.

What may non-fungible tokens be used for, and how do they work?

Most of people are skeptical about whether or not there are applications for NFTs. However, despite the idea being still in its infancy, many possible applications have already been identified. We've selected a few of the more noteworthy ones to include below:

Tickets

One of the applications of NFTs that we mentioned in our first step is the creation of event tickets. Essentially, if tickets are generated using a non-fungible token and a ticket is exchanged, a record of the transaction is established.

Consequently, there is zero possibility of someone scalping tickets, stealing tickets, or attempting to use forged tickets. This is due to the fact that there is no way to replace the token on a blockchain that is connected with that ticket.

Fashion

The use of NFTs in the fashion sector may help to solve a couple of key problems in the business. Having a digital record of authenticity, for starters, may be useful in dealing with problems such as counterfeit products. It is possible that luxury goods will come with an NFT affixed to prove that they are authentic.

Additionally, a non-fungible token may include critical information about the object's origins, such as the materials used, where they were obtained from, and how far the item has traveled since its creation. It is possible that this will assist individuals in making more ethical choices when concerns such as fashion and sustainability become more prominent.

Collectables

We've previously touched on this subject a little bit. People have long loved collecting mementos, trinkets, and other such things, and this has continued until the present. Authenticity is ensured via the use of NFTs, which act as a sort of digital signature or stamp of approval.

Gaming

In our piece on the video games business, we discussed the enormous market value associated with gaming and the use of NFTs to offer players a means of owning unique in-game goods. Such tokens may be used to fuel in-game ecosystems for a variety of reasons, including for entertainment, authenticity, and competition.

How to create an NFT

As a young digital artist, you may be interested in incorporating NFTs into your artwork. Fortunately, there are a variety of platforms accessible to assist you in getting started. The procedure is, on the whole, pretty straightforward, and the different platforms will help you through it.

Prior to getting started, though, there are a few things you should be aware of:

- Non-fiat tokens (NFTs) are based on and backed by a specific blockchain. In terms of non-fungible tokens, the Ethereum blockchain is presently the most widely used one.
- You'll need to have a cryptocurrency wallet, as well as cryptocurrency to use with it. Currently, ether is the most frequently utilized of these substances (ETH).
- NFT marketplaces allow you to produce and sell digital assets, which you can find here. For example, the OpenSea platform built on the Ethereum blockchain is a popular platform.

The pros and cons of NFTs

As a result, non-fungible tokens are obviously in vogue at the moment. But what exactly are the pros and cons of NFTs? We've listed some of the possible advantages and disadvantages below:

NFTs provides a number of advantages.

Some of the benefits of NFTs that are often mentioned are as follows:

- **They provide artists with ownership rights over digital creations**. A non-profit trust (NFT) provides content producers with the opportunity to demonstrate authenticity and benefit from their work once it has been created. When it comes to something like memes, which are widely distributed, this may result in a substantial revenue stream for the author.

- **They are one-of-a-kind and collectible**. Collecting something that is one-of-a-kind or uncommon is something that many individuals love since it provides them with a thrill. In addition, nationally recognized trademarks (NFTs) provide an additional degree of validity to collectible material, especially when it comes to digital assets.

- **They are unchangeable**. It is impossible to modify, delete, or replace non-fungible tokens due to the blockchain technology that underpins them. Once again, this is a useful feature when it comes to establishing the origin or legitimacy of digital material.

- **They have the capability of incorporating smart contracts**. In addition to smart contracts, another aspect of blockchain technology that is very interesting is decentralized ledgers. To put it an alternative way, they are capable of storing instructions that be performed when certain circumstances are fulfilled. Thus, an NFT with a smart contract might provide artists with a portion of the earnings if the NFT were to be resold at a later date.

The Downsides of NFTs Of course, there are certain possible drawbacks to be aware of like with any new technology. The following are some of the drawbacks of NFTs: • It is a speculative market. The major issue is still whether or not there is any real value in non-financial tokens. Do they represent a long-term investment? Or is it just a trend that will go away? It's difficult to tell. Currently, the only thing that gives NFTs their worth is their emotional character.

- **It is possible to copy digital materials**. Just because someone controls the non-transferable portion of a digital item does not rule out the possibility of duplicates of the asset. Graphics and movies may be copied and pasted, GIFs can be reshared hundreds of times, and art can be uploaded on a variety of websites. Just because you possess the NFT does not indicate that you have power over the asset - you just have a proof of ownership and validity.

- **The expenses associated with the environment**. Numerous discussions concerning the environmental effects of blockchain-based cryptocurrencies such as Ether and Bitcoin have taken place in recent years. To input entries into a blockchain, a significant amount of computer power is required. The issue of whether assets based on blockchain technology are long-term is a hotly debated topic.

- **They are susceptible to theft**. NFT technologies are reasonably secure; however, many of the exchanges and platforms that support them are not so safe. As an outcome, there have been many instances of NFTs being stolen as a result of cyber security breaches.

Is it possible that non-fungible tokens will become the norm in the future?

It is hoped that you now have a better grasp of what NFTs are and how they function. We've seen that non-fungible tokens have a variety of real-world uses, but are they a technology that'll be around for a long time?

It's difficult to predict whether or not NFTs will become more extensively utilized in the next years. Clearly, there is lots of interest in them at the present and a number of potential advantages. However, although the technology is still in its early stages, there remains a slew of difficulties to solve.

How to make and sell an NFT

What is the best way to manufacture and sell an NFT? Most likely, you've heard about them in the news, and maybe, despite the controversy surrounding them, you believe they could provide a means for you to earn money from your own creative work. We'll take you through the procedure step-by-step in this section of the site.

First and foremost, though, is a dose of realism. Although you may have heard of individuals selling NFTs for thousands of dollars (see our greatest NFT artwork article for a few examples), these are very uncommon occurrences and should be avoided. And even if you duplicate that accomplishment, the vast majority of the funds will not be distributed to you. This is because of the large number of costs that are paid to NFT artists, both before and after the sale, by the cryptocurrency businesses that allow the transactions and the platforms that create and manage the NFT. The fees are collected both upfront and after the sale. See our explanation on what is an NFT if you need some assistance understanding how they operate in more detail.

Often, the true nature of these fees will not become apparent until after you have already paid a sum of money. Furthermore, it is very probable that you will wind up losing money rather than earning it. One such example is Alan Gannett's explanation in this article on OneZero.com of how he produced four NFTs, sold one, and suffered a loss of over $1,000 as a result of the transaction. With that caution out of the way, continue reading to learn how to manufacture and trade NFT.

How to manufacture and market a non-functional toy

Please continue reading if you are prepared to accept the risk of learning how to navigate an NFT platform in its practical form. We've decided to illustrate this via the use of the NFT platform Rarible and the cryptocurrency platform MetaMask only for the sake of illustration. In no way does this imply an endorsement of either service, and there are many alternative options to explore.

Axie Marketplace and NFT ShowRoom are among the various non-financial-transaction (NFT) platforms available. Other payment systems available include Torus, Portis, WalletConnect (Coinbase), MyEtherWallet (MyEtherWallet), and Fortmatic (Fortmatic is a cryptocurrency exchange).

01. You'll need some bitcoin to get started.

With the purpose of understanding how NFTs work, you must first understand that you will be required to pay a platform in order to "mine" (i.e., create) one of them. And most sites require that this be paid in Ether, the native cryptocurrency of the open source blockchain platform Ethereum, as well as other digital currencies.

The value of Ether (abbreviated as ETH) may vary dramatically, similar to the value of Bitcoin, another prominent cryptocurrency, and other cryptocurrencies. As an example, at the time of writing this article, 1 ETH was worth $2,751.61 / £1,923.66 at the time of writing. However, the exchange rate had moved to $2,560.92 (£1,807.47) in less than five hours. As a result, if you're hoping to be able to predict exact numbers for your expenses and profits, you may as well give up on that idea.

To purchase Ethereum, you must first establish what is known as a 'digital wallet,' which you must then link to your preferred NFT platform of choice. There are a plethora of digital wallet services available, but for the sake of this article, we'll focus on MetaMask, which is accessible as both a browser extension and a mobile application.

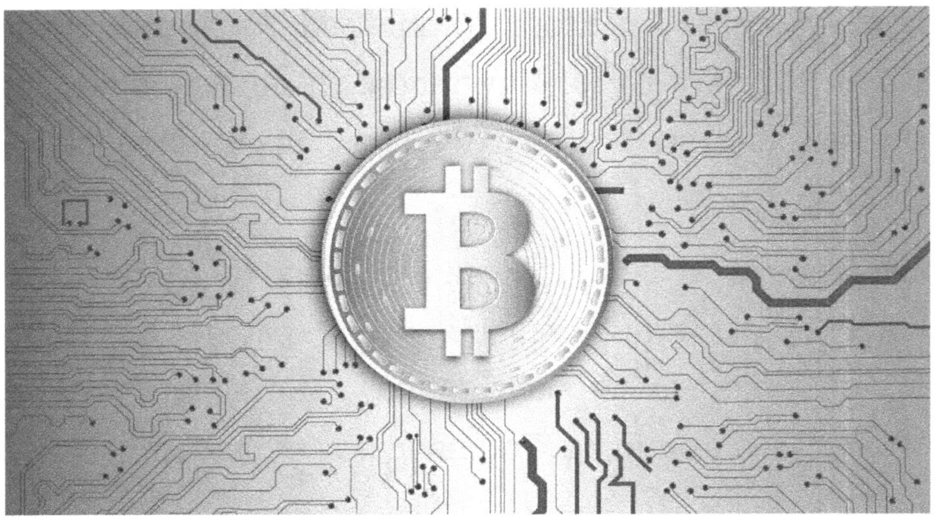

02. Create a digital wallet to store your valuables.

To use MetaMask to build a digital waller, go to the website and click on the blue 'Download' icon in the top-right corner of the screen. Given that we're working on a desktop computer, we'll select the browser extension option.

Following that, you'll be prompted to confirm that you want to 'establish a new wallet and seed phrase.' It is not essential to understand what a 'seed phrase' is, but in general, it is a collection of words that is used to store blockchain information on a computer.

That's something you should agree to. After then, it's simply a question of agreeing to the conditions, establishing a password, and going through some tiresome security procedures to have your account created and ready to use.

03. Make a deposit into your wallet.

Now that you've created a MetaMask wallet, it's time to fund it with some

Ethereum. This part is straightforward: just click on the 'Buy' button and then pick the option 'Buy ETH using Wyre' from the drop-down menu. Afterward, you'll be sent to a page where you may purchase ETH using either Apple Pay or a debit card.

04. Link your wallet to the NFT platform using the provided instructions.

Other wallets have a tendency to function in a similar manner. Once you've deposited some ETH into your wallet of choice, it's time to go over to the NFT platform itself and consume some of your funds. Although we'll utilize the Rarible platform for demonstration reasons, as we stated before, there are various NFT platforms available.

Go to Rarible.com to find out more. It will be located in the upper right-hand corner of the screen and will be labeled 'Connect wallet'. Following that, the following page asks you to enter the name of your wallet provider, which in our instance is MetaMask.

The option to link your wallet with Rarible will now show in a popup window, which you may choose to do. Click on 'Next,' then 'Connect,' then confirm that you are above the age of thirteen and that you have read and accepted the terms of service.

05. Place your file on the server.

Hooray! You're all set to start working on your NFT. To start, go to Rarible.com and click on the blue 'Create' icon located at the top right of the page. Your choices are either to create a single, one-time production or to sell the same thing on a number of occasions. In this case, we'll choose the option

'Single.'

Alternatively, you may upload the digital file you want to convert to an NFT at this point. For example, a PNG, GIF, WEBP, MP4 or MP3 file up to 30MB in size may be uploaded to Rarible, and it is free to do so.

We've produced a hilariously awful piece of art to serve as an illustration, which was inspired by David Hockney's latest contentious work. Upload your (hopefully much improved) digital file, and you'll get a sample of what your NFT post will look like on the right.

06. Hold an auction to raise funds.

In the next section of the form, you'll be asked to choose the method through which you want to sell your NFT artwork. You have three choices in this situation. When you use the term "fixed price," it means that you may establish a price and sell it immediately to someone (similar to the term "Buy it now" on eBay). When you have a 'Unlimited Auction,' individuals will continue to place bids until you accept one. Finally, an auction that takes place just for the duration of the specified period is known as a "timed auction." That's the choice we'll use as an example in this section.

The next step is the most difficult: determining a minimum price. It's important not to set it too low since the huge fees will eat up all of your earnings and may even cause you to lose money. Therefore, we'll set our price at a lofty 1 ETH and allow people seven days to submit bids for the cryptocurrency.

Following that, you'll see an option to 'Unlock once bought' on the form. This provides you with the opportunity to offer your eventual buyer with a complete, high-resolution version of your work, as well as extra content, via the use of a hidden web page or download link.

Below that is the choice that is the most difficult to understand on the form, labeled 'Choose Collection.' What you're requesting is a highly technical question regarding the way the blockchain is configured. The default setting for this field is 'Rarible,' and we recommend that you leave it that way.

07. Describe your NFT in detail.

After that, you will be able to customize your listing by adding a title and description. You'll need to spend some time improving this if you want to increase your chances of selling your NFT.

After that, you'll be asked to decide what proportion of royalties you'd want to receive from any future sales of your artwork. Another delicate balancing act, since although a larger percentage may earn you more money each sale, it will also discourage people from reselling your artwork in the first place because they will be more unlikely to make a profit for themselves.

Finally, there is an optional area where you may enter the characteristics of your file. After that, you're nearly finished.

08. Make a payment for the cost (but be warned)

Select 'Create Item' and you will be asked to login with your wallet in order to pay for the listing fee (if applicable). In the event that you do not have adequate money in your wallet, do not be concerned: you will not be required to restart. Instead, if you go to the top-right corner of the screen and click on the wallet symbol, you'll be presented with the opportunity to add money straight to your Rarible account.

But, before you do, take note of the following warning. The listing cost may seem to be insignificant: in our instance, it was just $5.91. However, this is just the beginning of the charges that you will be subjected to. Before proceeding any further, you must consent to a separate charge for the actual generation of your NFT, which in our case would have been $42.99 in our instance. In addition, there will be commission fees on the sale and transaction fees on the transfer of money from the buyer's wallet to your own wallet if someone really buys your NFT at the end of the transaction. As far as we could figure out, none of this was made particularly apparent on Rarible's website at the time we attempted to use it.

The complexity of blockchain technology, the wild fluctuations in cryptocurrency values, and the lack of transparency on the platforms themselves make it impossible to provide a clear and simple explanation of how to calculate the cost of generating and selling an NFT. However, we'd like to be able to do so in the future. So, if you make a sale, you'll have to wait and see how much you'll be charged in total as a result of the transaction.

CHAPTER 4

Digital Art and Digital Creators

Paints and brushes are some of the tools that some painters utilize to produce their artwork. However, today, many others utilize contemporary methods of developing their creativity, such as video technology, television, and computers, to further their own interests. Digital art is the term used to describe this kind of artwork.

Digital art is any work created or presented using digital technology, whether or not it was originally created using digital technology. Image types that fall under this category include pictures created entirely on a computer as well as hand-drawn drawings that are scanned into a computer and completed using software such as Adobe Illustrator. It is also possible to create digital art via animation and 3D virtual sculpting representations and projects that use many different technologies. Some digital art is created by manipulating video pictures in some way.

The phrase "digital art" was originally used in the 1980s to refer to a computer painting software that was developed at the time. To be clear, this was far back when they weren't even called applications! It may potentially be seen in many different ways, including on television and the Internet, on desktops, and on various social media platforms, making it a technique of art-making that lends itself to multi-media presentation. In a nutshell, digital art is a kind of fusion of the arts and technologies in certain ways. It opens them a plethora of new possibilities for artistic expression.

Historical Development

In 1965, artist Frieder Nake used an ER 56 computer (about the size of a typical room in a home) to apply an algorithm to analyze a Paul Klee picture. This is considered to be the "beginning of digital art." The artist produced many versions of "Highroads Byroads," and he called the one that, in his opinion, was the most effective Hommage à Paul Klee. Several artists and computer scientists collaborated over the same time period to develop computer-generated artworks, and the emphasis shifted to programming throughout the 1970s, allowing art to be made rather than merely copied or translated. The invention of the stylus enabled artists to use their inherent skills on computers, and it distinguished work that was computer-generated from work that was computer-aided in the production of the work. As a generation of artists started to alter video, music, and graphics in the 1980s, the field of digital media saw rapid development. By the early 2000s, the rapid expansion of computer usage has enabled artists to broaden their audience via the use of digital technology.

What Do Digital Artists Do for a Living?

Digital artists have a number of different professional options from which to select. Many of these jobs include creating visual effects and animated visuals for a variety of media, such as videos and computer games, among others. Digital artists may find employment in a variety of industries, including film production, advertising, video game development, and software creation. You will utilize computer software to bring your work to life, whether it be a painting or a sculpture, in any position involving digital artists. Depending on your profession, they may subsequently be transformed into 3D interactive graphics for websites or visual characters for animation. Specializations include game design, web design, multimedia, and animation, to name a few areas of interest. Whatever field you choose to work in, the ability to think creatively is essential.

How to Become a Digital Artist

Digital artists must have creative ability and a bachelor's degree in visual or commercial art, or in a related area, to succeed in their careers. Despite the fact that a degree is not required, this is a competitive profession, and it is essential to include formal training to both your CV and your portfolio to stand out. You must also keep up with the latest developments in creative and animation technologies. If you are unable to transfer your creative abilities from a pen and paper to a drawing tablet, entering the digital art industry may be challenging. The opportunity to do an internship in your chosen profession is a fantastic way to acquire practical experience, develop your abilities, and network with others in the industry.

What Software Do Digital Artists Use?

Digital artists utilize a wide variety of software tools to create their works. These may vary depending on your area of expertise, but the most popular are found inside the Adobe Creative Cloud. You may use Adobe InDesign to plan up print projects such as brochures, ebooks, posters, and magazines, as well as digital projects such as websites. Photoshop is one of the most popular photo-editing applications, and it may be used to enhance the appearance of your artwork. Adobe Illustrator, on the other hand, is the most essential software for 2D art. This is the stage at which you actually sketch and create your designs. If you work in Maya, animation and Harmony, which are not part of the Adobe Creative Cloud, are utilized for 2D and 3D animation. Harmony and Maya are not part of the Adobe Creative Cloud. Similarly to how your duties vary with your sector, so does the software that you need.

What's the Difference Between a Digital Artist and a Graphic Designer?

It is essential to note that there are significant distinctions between digital artists and graphic designers. A digital artist is concerned first and foremost with art, while a graphic designer is concerned first and foremost with conveying a message, which may include the use of various fonts, graphics, and pictures, as well as sound in certain instances. Design graphic designers work in advertising or for companies to develop layouts for advertisements, print projects, newsletters, and social media campaigns, all while keeping the target audience in mind. Being aware of your target audience has an impact on your decisions about color, style, and images to utilize in the project.

CHAPTER 5

Crypto Art

What is Crypto Art?

Crypto art is a kind of digital art that is growing in popularity. It is regarded in the same way as real artwork collections, and owners may be able to prove they are the fair owners of a piece of crypto art. Paintings or sculptures in private collections have long been part of the established structures in the art world.

However, despite the fact that it had been created, there was no obvious method for individuals to gather digital artwork until today. Cryptography and non-financial tokens (NFTs) enable you to do exactly that.

Cryptographic art may take various forms, ranging from digital images to music, virtual reality dreamscapes, and programmable art, to name a few. These digital assets may have a monetary worth to a collector and can represent a variety of things, including still graphic pictures, photography, GIFs, films, music, and other types of media.

The notion of digital scarcity underpins the creation of cryptographic artwork. With this frame of mind, you regard digital art as if it were a tangible product, and you purchase, sell, trade, and collect it like you would any other. Crypto Art, like conventional art, is only available in limited numbers, and in certain instances, purchasers may acquire the rights to partial royalties and the reproduction of the artwork in addition to the artwork itself.

Crypto art is often digital artwork, but it may also be actual artwork that has been recorded in a blockchain or "crypto" system. Thus, Crypto art is a term that refers to both digital and physical artwork. There are many crypto-themed artworks accessible in the cryptocurrency art niche and works with subject themes centered on digital culture and technology.

These artworks often contain themes related to contemporary politics, blockchain technology, cryptocurrencies, and its economics and philosophy. However, it is also feasible to publicly register and validate physical artworks via the use of cryptographic technology in certain circumstances. In addition, the use of blockchain technology may assist in distinguishing genuine artwork from counterfeit and establishing the ownership of an artwork.

How can I start selling my crypto art?

If you want to sell your work, there are a number of cryptocurrency art markets where you may do so. To compare it to individual eBays, think of all of these sites as auction houses where you may sell items for a set amount or have collectors bid on them. The one disadvantage is that most of these sites are a bit of a walled garden, where you must apply and be approved into these invite-only platforms before you can participate. Some are simple to enter, such as Async.art (which is a programmable art marketplace) and Rarible, while others are very difficult. Sites such as KnownOrigin, SuperRare, and Nifty Gateway (where Beeple sells) are very popular and have a large community of creators, but they are extremely difficult to be admitted into due to their strict admissions policies. However, OpenSea is the biggest platform for crypto art, where anybody may simply mint their own non-traditional works of art (NFTs) without the need of being approved. On OpenSea, you may also purchase items from the SuperRare, KnownOrigin, and MakersPlace collections.

Ethereum For Crypto Art

One of the most essential aspects of crypto art is that it is purchased and sold using a particular kind of cryptocurrency known as Ether (ETH). Ether is the cryptocurrency associated with the Ethereum blockchain, which is where NFTs are housed. Consider Ether to be similar to gambling chips. Each casino has its own unique chip, which you must purchase with money in order to use as currency to pay, play, and receive payments in that particular casino. Of course, you may also cash out your winnings at any time, just as you would with casino chips, to receive your money back. Some sites enable you to purchase crypto art using credit cards, but if you decide to sell it, you'll always get ETH in exchange, which you'll have to convert back into whatever non-crypto currency you choose.

Setting Up Your Crypto Wallet

A crypto art marketplace requires you to create an account and link it to a crypto wallet before you can begin selling your work. You need a cryptocurrency wallet because, in order to be able to sell or acquire crypto art, you must have a financing source from which you can withdraw cryptocurrency or into which you can deposit cryptocurrency. Therefore, these sites will need you to establish a wallet via either MetaMask or

Fortmatic, after which you'll be able to connect the wallet to your marketplace account.

Your cryptocurrency wallet must be fully funded with Ethereum before you can begin selling. "Wait, I'm supposed to have money in order to sell my cryptographic artwork?" Yes, you are right. The tokenization/minting of each item sold in order for it to be placed on the blockchain is required every time it is sold. Minting is the act of authenticating your artwork so that it can be tracked and traced back to its original owner at any point in time. In addition, gas costs, which are associated with this minting procedure, must be paid using Ethereum in order to complete the transaction. It is essentially the energy cost for all the machines involved in computing the transaction and tokenizing your labor that is charged as gas fees. These gas costs are subject to change and fluctuation at any time in response to changes in computational demand. And you thought the idea of cryptographic art was difficult to grasp!

Getting Ethereum For Crypto Art

You must pay for these gas costs using Ethereum (ETH), which you must have in your crypto wallet before you can use them. So, how do you go about getting ETH to put in said cryptocurrency wallet? Sites like as Coinbase are well-known for facilitating the exchange of fiat currency (such as the US dollar) for cryptocurrencies. By registering for a Coinbase account, you'll be able to create a Coinbase wallet, which you may then use to transfer money from your bank or Paypal account. After that, all you have to do is trade your USD into ETH. In order to mint your first piece, you will need to transfer money from your Coinbase wallet to your Metamask/Formatic crypto wallet, which is connected to your marketplace account.

Dropping Your Fir

You've prepared your cryptocurrency wallet and are ready to sell your first piece of cryptocurrency! What should I do now? Marketplaces enable you to submit a variety of file types, whether you're looking to sell a static picture, an animation, or even an interactive augmented reality experience. Then it's quite similar to the process of selling anything on eBay. Set your "Buy It Now" price—or minimum bid price, if you want collectors to be able to bid on your art—after you've written a description and included tags. You may also specify a time restriction for how long your item will be available for purchase. Next, you may sell a single copy of your work, referred to as a "edition," or many editions of the same item. The greater the number of editions you produce, the less valuable a work may become. Then you may tokenize and mint your piece (think of it as digitally signing your work), and you can start working on the next step: creating your first drop. A drop is the term utilized to describe the act of placing your cryptoart up for sale. As soon as you have dropped, you may sit back and relax until the ETH comes in.

How To Sell Your Crypto Art (Selling Out In Style)

The payment for your artwork will be made in ETH, which will be transferred into the crypto wallet that you linked to the marketplace where your piece was sold. This money may then be kept in your wallet or transferred to a currency trading platform like as Coinbase for conversion to USD or any other non-cryptocurrency. The price of ETH is highly volatile, changing minute by minute, similar to that of Bitcoin, where the price is very variable. To give you an example, when I sold my first NTF, the Maneki Neko shown above, I received 1.5 (1.5 Ether), which at the time was worth about $620. At the time of writing this post, one cent is worth more than

$1,350. As a result, whether you retain your profits in ETH or pay them out in a non-cryptocurrency is always a decision.

How Can I Make Money with Cryptocurrency? Picasso, don't go so fast.

Cryptography is not a get-rich-quick scam in any way shape or form. Most crypto art is simply sold for a few bucks. In this sense, the crypto art world is similar to the conventional art world, in that it is controlled by a small number of individuals who are very successful and earn a lot of money from their work. This is due to wealthy individuals diversifying their assets, and you can see the same thing happening in the realm of digital art. The world is very much like the Wild West when it comes to earning money off unprofessional-looking shiny spherical animations. You'll see artists you've probably never heard of making a lot of money off animations that seem amateurish. On the other hand, fine art is likely to have caught your eye and made you wonder why someone spent thousands of dollars for it. I'm referring to you, the banana that was duct taped to a wall.

In the case of someone who had an online presence before to crypto art (such as Beeple), you have a ready-made audience that is more than likely eager to purchase your work. However, is it possible for collectors to discover your crypto art if studios can't find it online to employ you? Sure, if you don't have a lot of exposure, you're not going to earn much (if any) money selling cryptocurrency art. However, although producing and sharing a large amount of work may have the unintended consequence of increasing your exposure, which may assist you in securing your next client job, or at the very least improve your abilities and assist you in discovering your creative voice.

What Kind Of Cryptocurrency Are You Looking For?

Popular crypto art seems to have a distinct aesthetic, but it does not imply that you will be successful if you attempt to copy what is currently popular. Maintain your integrity. Work on the project that you're going to put your heart and soul into, and put out your best effort to produce the things that you want to do and are enthusiastic about producing. Finally, pay attention to your inner voice. The more you do it, the more others will notice it, and the more it will connect with them.

New technologies almost always have significant flaws that must be worked out. When it comes to producing cryptographic art, there is one important aspect to keep in mind. Keep in mind that crypto art is stored on the Ethereum blockchain. It requires a tremendous number of computations to implement blockchain technology, which necessitate even greater demands on the environment. Furthermore, the present paradigm is very detrimental to the environment. This implies that, yes, when you produce cryptographic art, you contribute to energy use. In order to move the Ethereum blockchain towards a more sustainable route (referred to as Ethereum 2.0), work is now being done to decrease energy usage by 99 percent (see Ethereum 2.0).

Can I Really Be Successful in Crypto Art?

Take it this way: artists are already producing personal work and spec work, either because they love the process of creating or in the expectation that a customer would someday discover their work, employ them and pay their fees. Why not try your hand at producing art in the hopes that a collector would find it compelling enough to want to invest in your career and support you by purchasing your work?

"Would you want to invest in me?" you could ask.

Yes, it is possible to conceive about it in this manner. Cryptographic art has the appearance of being an investment. In this case, rather of needing to be like a business that goes public, you may be an artist who people will invest in. It's similar to a primary public offering (IPO), only that motion designers are the company that is going public. Another thing to keep in mind is that cryptographic art has a history of increasing in value year after year, with an average annual rise of about 7 percent.

According to my own experience, the minute someone purchases your first piece of cryptographic art, your whole attitude changes. And let's just call it a day.

CHAPTER 6

NFT and Blockchain

A blockchain is a distributed software network that acts as a digital record as well as a method for the safe transfer of assets without the need for a third party to act as an intermediary. Similar to how the internet enables the digital flow of information, blockchain is a technology that allows the digital exchange of units of value in the same way that the internet promotes the movement of information. For example, on a blockchain network, anything from money to land titles to votes may be tokenized, stored, and traded, and this includes votes themselves.

The Bitcoin blockchain, a peer-to-peer electronic currency system that is safe, censorship-resistant, and decentralized, was the first manifestation of blockchain technology, appearing in 2009. Bitcoin is an example of an open, or permissionless, blockchain, since it is available to anybody who wants to use it.

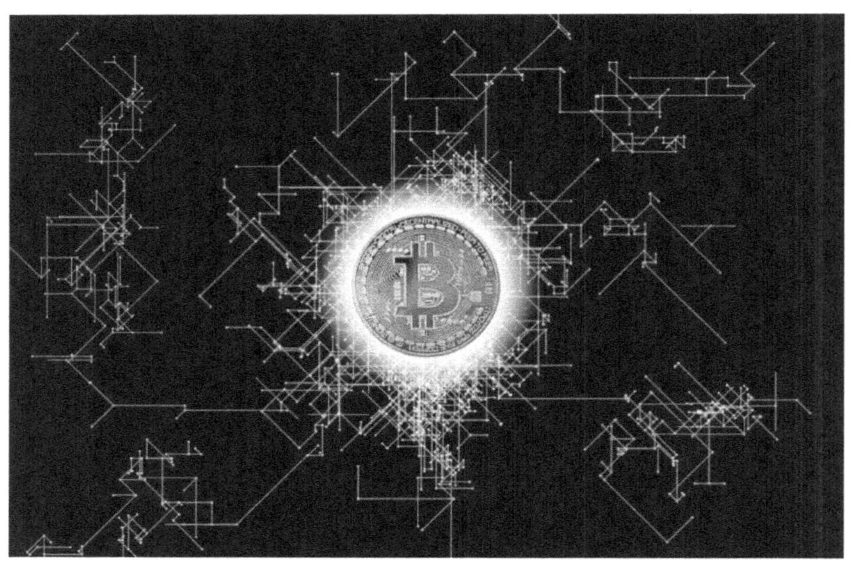

There are several different types of blockchain technology available today.

Some blockchains have been created to suit the requirements of a small number of players, and access to the network is limited for these individuals. These are instances of permissioned blockchains, which are private blockchains.

Blockchain technology, in addition to ensuring the safe movement of money, creates a permanent forensic record of all transactions as well as a single version of the truth - a network state that is completely visible and presented in real time for the benefit of all players.

However, regardless of the type of blockchain protocol implemented, blockchain technology holds great promise for transforming centuries-old business models, leading the way for higher levels of legitimacy in government, and opening up new avenues for economic opportunity for everyday citizens.

NFT

The fact that Saturday Night Live includes a sketch on non-fungible tokens indicates that the idea has reached a broad audience. Many people's reactions to NFTs were recorded by Saturday Night Live, including bewilderment, disbelief, and eye rolling. NFTs, on the other hand, are here to stay and will play an increasingly significant part in our digital economy as time goes on. In other words, what exactly are they, and how do they fit into the blockchain ecosystem?

Remember that a blockchain is a piece of software that serves as a ledger and is spread among nodes of a communications network. It is not a cryptocurrency. The immutability of the blockchain differentiates it from other online databases or trading platforms: we may exchange digital assets peer to peer, and no one can modify or reverse those transactions without the permission of a majority of the network. That's a significant advantage when communicating over the Internet.

At one end of the range of digital assets are cryptocurrencies such as bitcoin, which are used -such as the Bitcoin blockchain- in payment networks, and at the other end are digital assets such as e-gold. In other words, bitcoins are fungible, which means that one bitcoin is equivalent in value and function to every other bitcoin in the system. You may thus swap one bitcoin with another without violating the conditions of your contract if you have a contract involving bitcoins.

NFTs are at the opposite end of the spectrum: each token represents a unique item with a high monetary value. In a contract, you couldn't just swap out an Andrew Wyeth painting for a piece by Mike Winkelmann and expect no one to notice the difference. Nationally unique assets (NFTs) include valuables and birth and death certificates, titles of property, and the identities of devices connected to the Internet of Things (IoT).

However, although the hype around CryptoKitties, the initial NFT craze, has subsided, the excitement surrounding the auction of Beeple's work has highlighted the possibilities of NFTs in the future. You are only limited by your imagination, your technical ability to generate value in that area, and your capacity to get marketing, accounting, and legal assistance to see it through to completion.

CHAPTER 7

NFT as Collectibles and Digital Assets

What exactly is an NFT, and why is it becoming such a big issue in the press these days? Cryptographic tokens known as non-fungible tokens (also known as non-fungible tokens) enable someone to verify that an online asset is the genuine article. 2020 was a banner year for the cryptocurrency industry, and the subject of decentralized finance has only gained in prominence, with companies such as Tesla investing significant sums of money in cryptocurrencies and Bitcoin hitting all-time highs, among other things. Since the end of 2020, there has been a continuous increase in the popularity and usage of NFTs, which have sold for millions of dollars in some instances.

Cryptocurrencies such as Bitcoin are referred to be 'fungible' tokens since they are interchangeable and do not have a unique serial number. Therefore, if you were to trade one Bitcoin for another, you would be receiving basically the identical item. Each coin is identical to the others in terms of design. Non-fungible tokens, on the other hand, indicate something that is one-of-a-kind and cannot be replaced. An NFT may be stamped onto, for example, an original GIF or picture as evidence that the item being traded or sold is the genuine one. This is similar to trading or selling an original artwork that has been authenticated. Another way of putting it is that an NFT is a cryptographic token that enables someone to verify that an online asset is genuine. Because of this, resources are scarce, which in principle leads to the creation of value, even in the digital realm, where assets are not physically present.

Maintaining the security of your NFTs

Given the potential worth of NFTs, it is only reasonable to consider the issue of protecting these digital assets from being compromised. Are they completely safe to use? In general, purchasing and holding non-fiat currencies (NFTs) is just as safe as purchasing and holding bitcoin. However, even though the technology that underpins NFTs is considered to be secure, there are certain precautions you should take to guarantee the safety of your investment. Here are some suggestions for keeping NFTs safe:

1. **Select a safe and secure wallet**. NFTs, like cryptocurrencies, are saved and utilized via the use of a cryptocurrency wallet. The wallet you choose is critical in this regard, since certain wallets are more trustworthy and safe than others. For example, a wallet that keeps your private key exclusively on your device, needs strong passwords, supports two-factor authentication, encrypts your data, and requires you to set up a recovery passphrase are all desirable features.

   Hacken, a cybersecurity firm specializing in blockchain technology, conducted a case study examining nine non-custodial wallets. Based on different factors, including whether or not each wallet published their third-party audit results, whether or not each wallet requires strong passwords, and whether or not each wallet has a history of security breaches, they determined that Metamask and Enjin are the safest wallets available. For a more detailed description of the technique utilized, as well as a list of wallets, please visit this page.

1. **Make your password difficult to guess**. You've probably noticed that you're using the same password for many different accounts. Please, don't do that! A long, one-of-a-kind, and difficult password is required for your wallet. Pro tip: This recommendation should be followed for each and every account you have.

2. **Enable two-factor authentication on your computer**. Two-factor authentication, just like it does with your bitcoin wallet, is very beneficial. Due to the need for authentication prior to performing operations, the likelihood of an NFT being stolen or mistakenly given to someone decreases significantly.

3. **Make a note of your recovery phrase and keep it somewhere safe**. In the event that you forget your password, your passphrase will serve as a final option for regaining access to your account. If you are using a mnemonic phrase, be certain that your passphrase is not readily guessable and that it is kept in a safe place. You will very certainly be unable to restore your account if you forget your recovery phrase.

4. **Make frequent backups of your wallet**. In the case of a system malfunction or the loss of a device, you can be certain that you will be capable to restore your data. It is a good idea to keep many backups of your data.

5. **Make sure to keep your software up to date**. Security patches are included in software upgrades.

6. **Make use of a protected internet connection**. An attacker will have an easier time stealing your information if you use a public wifi network. If you must use public wifi, use a virtual private network (VPN) to protect your connection and turn off the bluetooth connection on your device.

In addition to these measures, it is important to be aware of your legal rights in relation to your NFTs as well. Although NFTs demonstrate that a particular piece of data is one-of-a-kind, they do not prohibit someone from tokenizing anything that is not their own. Fortunately, there are legal safeguards in place that you may take advantage of. For example, NFTs may be subject to standard copyright legislation. Using the Digital Millennium Copyright Act (DCMA)*, you might, for example, submit a takedown request against the platform selling and the producers of these NFTs if you think your digital work is being stolen.

CoinDesk also advises that you specify what you are offering to customers in your listing description. For example, what do you own if you hold the rights to a work you're selling? Do you own the underlying art (for example, an original GIF) or simply the digital representation of the work? Or, to put it another way, be precise on the front end by designing your smart contract to describe the rights that are being transferred when it is feasible or suitable.

CHAPTER 8

Common NFT Marketplaces

Here is a list of prominent NFT markets that feature a user-friendly interface, a significant amount of investor engagement, and a high volume of trading activity on them. It includes companies such as OpenSea, Rarible, SuperRare, Decentraland, and NBA Top Shot. The Ethereum blockchain network serves as the foundation for the first four NFT trading platforms. For example, NBA Top Shot is a blockchain-based application that operates effectively on the Flow blockchain platform.

Explore the features and functions of these five platforms in the sections below!

OpenSea

In terms of daily trading volume ($49.18 million), it is the most important NFT marketplace in the world. Artists who utilize the Polygon blockchain network, for example, no longer have to pay gas costs on the OpenSea platform, which is a novel concept (integrated with Ethereum).

The term "Lazy Minting" refers to the fact that sellers do not pay minting costs until and until their cryptocurrency collectible is sold to an interested investor. Accordingly, purchasers may acquire high-valued works of art such as domain names, music, sports items, trading cards, other utility assets, and other utility assets.

On the OpenSea platform, where may crypto aficionados keep their non-fungible tokens? They may utilise digital wallets like as Coinbase Wallet,

Dapper, MetaMask, Portis, Torus, Trust Wallet, WalletConnect, and WalletLink to store their cryptocurrency. As a result, individuals may safeguard their digital treasures by using passwords and private keys to do so.

Those interested in beginning their own business may buy an OpenSea replica. Additionally, they may quickly grow their user base by recruiting artists and investors.

Rarible

The Rarible NFT marketplace has received 188,884 crypto collectibles worth a total of $139.87 million in purchases, according to DAppRadar's statistics. What is the company's unique selling proposition (USP)? The Rarible Governance Token, which is built on the Ethereum blockchain network, is available to users (RGT).

There are a total of ten million Rari governance tokens available for purchase. Each holder is entitled to certain advantages, such as decision-making authority and voting rights. Other software wallets, such as Fortmatic and MyEtherWallet (MEW), may also be used by investors to store and back up their Non-Fungible Token holdings (NFTs). Syncing their email addresses, phone numbers, and social media profiles are all options available to them.

In addition, the Rarible NFT trading platform provides real-time information on hot bids, live auctions, and top collections from across the world. DeFi assets such as call options and treasury bonds and metaverses are also available for purchase by investors.

Techpreneurs may get a Rarible clone for a little fee. Additionally, it may sell a range of assets via auctions that are based on a bidding mechanism.

SuperRare

It is a well-known online marketplace for digital art. SuperRare's unique selling point is its emphasis on verifying each piece of material submitted by a content provider. In addition, NFT sellers earn royalties for every secondary sale of their artwork made via the NFT marketplace.

Today, the SuperRare NFT trading platform serves as a focal point for a wide range of art exhibits, initiatives, and limited-edition releases. In addition, three wallets are available to both content creators and investors (Fortmatic, MetaMask, and WalletConnect).

Furthermore, SuperRare saw a trading volume of $403,430 in the previous seven days. The NFT marketplace, which is built on Ethereum, has seen 383 users execute 668 peer-to-peer (P2P) transactions in the last week, according to DAppRadar data.

Decentraland

Have you ever been curious about a website that offers virtual parcels of land? Decentraland does this via the use of cutting-edge technologies such as 3D technology and Virtual Reality (VR).

MANA is also available for purchase by investors (an ERC-20 token). These tokens are burned in order to purchase the NFTs based on the ERC-721 protocol (LAND tokens). What is the best way for investors to make advantage of the valuable MANA token? They may purchase visually appealing avatars, names, and wearables.

In the Decentraland NFT marketplace, phrases such as "Incredible Structures," "Medieval Dungeon Maze," and "Virtual World" are used to describe the marketplace. artists may build artworks, challenges, and settings based on their own ideas Furthermore, those who participate in numerous events have the opportunity to earn interesting prizes and incentives.

On the Decentraland NFT trading platform, investors have placed a total of $26,280 in smart contracts that are compatible with Ethereum. Overall, it has succeeded in establishing a strong Decentralized Autonomous Organization (DAO) via the sale of land parcels and high-end real estate to interested investors.

NBA Top Shot

NFTs have always been about being one-of-a-kind. On the Flow blockchain network, the NBA Top Shot platform does this flawlessly.... It has attracted a large number of basketball enthusiasts via the sale of collections and packs (Starter and Booster).

The newest information on certified ballers, the most recent moments, the most valuable listings, and rare moments of both players and teams are sent to investors in real time. Users may choose from a variety of NFT levels, including Common, Fandom, Legendary, and Rare NFTs.

In addition, basketball fans may watch their favorite teams (from the Eastern Conference and Western Conference) in the NBA League, which is held in Las Vegas.

The NBA Top Shot NFT marketplace, which is particularly noteworthy, has sold more than 8.1 million crypto collectibles to 425,160 dealers so far. According to DAppRadar's statistics, the total trade volume has exceeded $655.99 million in total.

Those interested in starting their own NFT marketplace may buy white-label clone solutions from the aforementioned markets. Then, they may establish these custom-built trading platforms and generate substantial income through auction fees, bidding costs, gas fees, and transaction processing fees, among other sources.

Axie Marketplace

The NFT-driven video game Axie Infinity is home to the second-largest NFT marketplace, with a total trade volume of more than $2.1 billion on Dappradar, which the NFT powers. There are no other items for sale or trade on the Axie Marketplace other than Axies, which are adorable, Pokémon-like digital creatures that users may purchase and sell on the Axie Marketplace.

By using the built-in breeding mechanisms of the game, you can also generate new Axies that you can then sell on the Marketplace. The NFTs in Axie Infinity have a function as opposed to art NFTs, which are just gathered for the sake of collecting. You may use the NFTs in-game to fight monsters and other players, earning tokens that can be used to breed new species. NFTs from Axie Infinity have proved to be so profitable that some players in the Philippines and Indonesia have made a livelihood solely on the breeding and selling of NFTs from the company.

Axie Infinity, on the other hand, is one of the most difficult NFT services for new users to learn how to use, and you'll have to jump through a lot of hoops before you can even begin to enjoy yourself.

It is necessary to set up an Ethereum wallet, such as MetaMask, deposit Ethereum into Ronin, and purchase a minimum of three Axies from the Axie market in addition to using an Ethereum wallet (which will set you back several hundred dollars). Of course, this is not a desirable situation for the average person on the street, but it is not out of reach for a seasoned crypto user.

CryptoPunks/Larva Labs

CryptoPunks is a set of 10,000 randomly generated characters with a pixel art style and unique characteristics that was one of the first instances of non-fungible tokens (NFTs) on the Ethereum network. Unfortunately, even though they were initially available for free, now the only way to get one is to pay for it out of pocket.

That entails visiting the marketplace operated by CryptoPunks developer Larva Labs, where the vast bulk of purchases are made. Furthermore, purchasing a Punk is very expensive; presently, the lowest-priced Punk will set you back 94.99 ETH (about $285,000), while the most valued Punk ever sold on the marketplace (number 3100) changed hands for an absolutely ridiculous $7.58 million. That explains Larva Labs' total trading volume of $1.3 billion throughout the course of its history.

Start by connecting your MetaMask wallet, searching through the list of available Punks (those with red backgrounds are for sale), and placing your offer.

The most complicated aspect of the procedure is persuading yourself to part with such a ridiculous sum of money, but that is entirely your responsibility. After all, the cost of art is in the eye of the beholder.

KnownOrigin

It has a considerably lower total trade volume (only $6.9 million) than SuperRare. However, SuperRare seeks to offer the discriminating NFT enthusiast a more curated, gallery-like experience via its token KnownOrigin.

All of the company's artwork files are stored on IPFS, which offers a degree of security for the underlying digital assets. It's a marketplace that puts a heavy emphasis on digital art, and it stays away from more outlandish elements of the NFT universe, so don't expect to see any crazy avatars or adorable creatures here.

The usage of KnownOrigin is straightforward, even at the risk of sounding like a broken record. Just link your wallet, such as MetaMask or Formatic, and you'll be bidding on your own highly sought-after NFT assets in no time.

Foundation, which announces itself as a "creative playground" for artists, had a total trading volume of little more than $79 million at the time of writing. Among the noteworthy sales have been the first NFT of the famous Internet meme Nyan Cat, Edward Snowden's first NFT, and an audiovisual digital collectable produced by producer Richard D. James, best known under his stage as Aphex Twin.

Once you've linked your MetaMask or other software wallet to Foundation's marketplace via WalletConnect, the marketplace is straightforward to use, allowing you to make bids on timed auctions in the same way you would on a traditional auction site.

MakersPlace

MakingPlace is another boutique NFT marketplace that takes pleasure in housing many unique collections of digital fine art. It is also known for its high-quality customer service. Even while its overall volume ($23.5 million at the time of writing) is on the lower end of the spectrum, it includes a large number of one-of-a-kind works that contribute to its rarity.

In February 2021, the site was briefly downed after legendary crypto artist Beeple offered a collection of NFTs for $1 each, causing widespread outrage.

A number of NFT drops by artists have also taken place on the site, with the likes of T-Pain, Shakira, and Rage Against the Machine's Tom Morello among those who have joined up.

When you join up as a buyer at MakersPlace, the process is straightforward, and you can even connect in using your Google or Facebook accounts to save time.

As part of the registration procedure, you'll be required to choose five artists to follow, and you'll be able to buy their works using either your MetaMask ETH balance or (more conveniently) your credit card. If you're a creator, you'll need to seek an invitation to join the platform by filling out an online form and submitting it for approval by the site's curators.

Nifty Gateway

Nifty Gateway, one of the first wave of large NFT markets, has a strong sponsor in the shape of cryptocurrency exchange Gemini, which bought the platform back in April of this year. Although it was an untimely move, Nifty Gateway made news in February 2021 when it brokered the sale of Beeple's CROSSROAD for $6.6 million, making it one of the first multimillion-dollar NFT transactions to take place during the boom period. By the end of May, the platform's gross merchandise value had reached $300 million.

The website releases a carefully selected selection of NFT drops on a tri-weekly basis, with artists like The Weeknd, Grimes, and Eminem among those who contributed to the platform. A marketplace is also available where you may explore curated collections, confirmed artists, and a larger variety of work by unverified artists.

Final Thoughts

Above all, there is a great deal of anticipation for the growth of the NFT marketplace across the globe right now. As a result, a slew of new platforms, including Alibaba, Jumbish, NOWwhere, Rario, and Vibranium, have been established in nations such as China and India, among others.

The applications of cryptographic collectibles are also evolving. Several million dollars are being spent by investors on digital animals, memes, pebbles, and shoes, among other things. Additionally, copyright protection and protections against copying are being extended to artists as well.

Another set of NFT markets, such as Foundation, MakersPlace, Nifty Gateway, Sorare, and The Sandbox, are seeing tremendous growth in recent months. In addition, venture capitalists (VCs) are also putting money into the NFT trading platforms, which are a growing trend.

The simplicity with which crypto collectibles may be created, as well as gas costs, royalties, and security measures, will determine their long-term viability. Businesses may make the correct decision right now by contacting a firm that develops marketplaces for new financial technologies. They will be able to easily organize auctions, communicate directly with artists and investors, and pocket unimaginable amounts of money very quickly.

CHAPTER 9

How to Invest in NFT

<u>Steps to Invest in an NFT:</u>

1. Open an NFT Marketplace Account

You may browse via an online NFT marketplace without having to register for the platform. However, in order to use cryptocurrencies, you must first establish a digital wallet that will be financed with cryptocurrency. When you add your digital wallet to the online marketplace, it will automatically open your account. Following the completion of this process, you will be able to engage in the marketplace and make investments.

2. Create a digital wallet in order to purchase NFTs.

The functionality of a digital wallet is similar to that of a traditional wallet in that it stores your money, but a digital wallet is especially intended to store cryptocurrencies.

Generally speaking, a cold wallet, also known as a digital wallet that stores bitcoin on a thumb drive or other physical media, is the ideal option for most people. Because it will not be actively browsing the internet, it is less likely that the wallet will be hacked.

You'll need to get a digital wallet that is compatible with the NFT marketplace where you want to make your investment (for example, Open Sea works with Ethereum). This means that your wallet must be compatible with the cryptocurrency you want to purchase and sell on the site. For example, the cryptocurrency Ether is supported by MetaMask.

3. Make a deposit into your account.

To engage in an NFT marketplace, you must first purchase a cryptocurrency such as Ether.

Through investment brokers specializing in cryptocurrency trading, such as Webull and SoFi Active Invest, you may complete your transaction quickly and simply. Investing in individual stocks, exchange-traded funds (ETFs), and options is completely commission-free with each of these brokerages. However, they also provide the ability to buy famous cryptocurrencies like as Ether and Bitcoin.

Check out Gemini if you're looking for a cryptocurrency platform that's devoted to cryptocurrency trading. A cryptocurrency exchange offers a complete range of services, including buying, selling, and storing digital assets. Furthermore, being a cryptocurrency-specific website, Gemini provides a plethora of tools and research material to assist you in better understanding the cryptocurrency market.

The cryptocurrency you buy may be loaded into your digital wallet, which can then be used on an NFT marketplace once it has been purchased.

4. Purchase Your NFT

If you have a digital wallet that is operational and funded with bitcoin, you will be ready to purchase.

It is critical to realize that NFT markets operate on an auction basis. Therefore, it is necessary for you to place a bid on the token you want to buy. The transaction will go through as scheduled if you are either the highest bidder or the only bidder.

CHAPTER 10

NFT Stocks

Bitcoin and other cryptocurrencies, like real money, are fungible, which means that they may be traded or swapped for one another. For example, the value of one Bitcoin is always the same as the value of another Bitcoin. In a same vein, one unit of Ether is always equal to another unit of Ether. Because of their fungibility, cryptocurrencies are well-suited for use as a safe means of exchange in the digital economy, where they have gained widespread acceptance.

Due to the fact that each token is unique and irreplaceable, NFTs alter the cryptographic paradigm, making it impossible for one non-fungible token to be considered the same as another. Instead, they are digital representations of assets that have been compared to digital passports due to the fact that each token includes a unique, non-transferable identity that allows it to be distinguished from the other tokens in circulation. They are also extendable, which means that you may combine two NFTs to create a third, one-of-a-kind NFT by breeding them together.

NFTs, like Bitcoin, include ownership information that allows token holders to be easily identified and transferred between one another. In addition, NFTs allow asset owners to provide information or characteristics related to the item. For example, in the case of coffee beans, tokens representing the beans may be classed as fair trade. Alternatively, artists may sign their digital artwork by including their own signature in the information associated with it.

NFTs developed as a result of the ERC-721 standard. ERC-721 is a smart contract standard developed by some of the same individuals who were responsible for the ERC-20 smart contract standard. It defines the bare minimum interface – including ownership details, security, and metadata – that is necessary for the exchange and distribution of gaming tokens. Taking the idea a step further, the ERC-1155 standard lowers the transaction and storage costs associated with non-fungible tokens while also batching several kinds of non-fungible tokens into a single contract.

Cryptokitties, maybe the most well-known use of NFTs, are a good example. Cryptokitties, which were introduced in November 2017 and have unique identification numbers on the Ethereum blockchain, are digital representations of cats. Each cat is one-of-a-kind and has a corresponding ether value. They breed amongst themselves and create new offspring, each of whom has a unique set of characteristics and values compared to their parents. Following its debut, crypto kitties quickly gained a large following, with fans spending more than $20 million in ether to purchase, feed, and otherwise care for them in only a few short weeks. Some fans went so far as to spend upwards of $100,000 on the project.

While the crypto kitties use case may seem to be inconsequential, the ones that follow it have far-reaching economic ramifications. For example, non-financial transactions (NFTs) have been utilized in both private equity and real estate transactions. Thus, incorporating several kinds of tokens into a single contract has many ramifications, one of which being the potential to serve as an escrow for various forms of NFTs, ranging from artwork to real estate, in a single financial transaction.

The top three non-financial-transactions stocks

Here is a list of the three finest NFT stocks to invest in:

1. Mattel, Inc.

Playthings and other consumer products are the focus of Mattel, Inc., which was established in 1945 and is headquartered in California. It now has a market capitalization of $7.6 billion. According to the news outlet The New York Times, Reuters reported on June 17th that the company will shortly launch a limited sale of NFTs. In addition, an auction of three works of digital art utilizing NFTs based on the blockchain will take place.

2. Funko, Inc.

Funko, Inc., established in 2017, is a Washington-based company that manufactures and distributes pop culture consumer products. It has a market capitalization of $741 million and employs about 2,000 people. According to financial adviser Bank of America, the price objective for Funko shares has been increased from $12 to $30, which believes the company's core business is doing well.

3. PLBY Group

PLBY Group, Inc., established in 1953 and based in California, is a pleasure and leisure services company with a market capitalization of $1 billion. The company was founded in 1953 and operated from California. In addition, PLayboy (a lifestyle brand owned by the company) announced on July 9th that it will be collaborating with the Miami Beach Art Collection to exhibit NFT Art at the Miami Beach Art Collection. Immediately after the news, the stock price increased by 2 percent.

Why Are Non-Fungible Tokens Important?

In comparison to the relatively basic idea of cryptocurrencies, non-fungible tokens represent a significant advancement. Modern finance systems are comprised of complex trading and financing systems for a wide range of asset kinds, ranging from real estate to lending contracts to artwork, among other things. NFTs, by making it possible to create digital representations of physical assets, offer a significant step forward in the reinvention of this infrastructure.

To be sure, the concept of digital representations of real assets and the usage of unique identification are not new concepts. Nevertheless, when these ideas are coupled with the advantages of a tamper-resistant blockchain of smart contracts, they become a powerful force for positive change.

The efficiency of the market is perhaps the most apparent advantage of NFTs. A physical item that is converted into a digital asset simplifies procedures and eliminates the need for middlemen. The use of non-fungible tokens (NFTs) to represent digital or physical artwork on a blockchain eliminates the need for agents and enables artists to communicate with their audiences directly. They may also help to enhance the efficiency of corporate operations. For example, it will be simpler for various players in the supply chain to communicate with an NFT for a wine bottle, and it will aid in tracking the bottle's origin, manufacture, and sale throughout the whole process. A solution of this kind has previously been created by the consulting company Ernst & Young for one of its customers.

Non-fungible tokens are also ideal for use in the context of identification management. For example, consider the situation of actual passports, which must be shown at every entrance and departure point. When individuals' passports are converted into National Identification Cards, each with its own unique identifying features, it becomes possible to simplify the entrance and departure procedures for jurisdictions across the world. Furthermore, NFTs may be utilized for identity management in the digital world, which is an extension of the previous use case.

In addition, non-financial institutions (NFTs) may democratize investment by fractionalizing tangible assets such as real estate. For example, it is considerably simpler to split a digital real estate asset among numerous owners than it is to divide a physical real estate asset among many owners. This tokenization ethic does not have to be limited to real estate; it can be suitable to other types of assets as well, such as artwork. As a result, an artwork does not necessarily need a single owner. Instead, multiple people may own the artwork's digital counterpart, each of whom is accountable for a different portion of the painting. Such agreements have the potential to enhance the company's value and income.

The development of new markets and types of investment represents the most intriguing prospect for non-financial institutions. Think of a piece of real estate that has been subdivided into numerous divisions, each of which includes a distinct set of features and various kinds of property. It's possible that one of the divisions is located near a beach, while another is an entertainment complex, and still another is a residential neighborhood. An NFT represents a unique piece of land and each piece of land is valued differently based on its unique features. It is possible to make real estate dealing, which is a complicated and bureaucratic endeavor, more straightforward by integrating essential information into each individual NFT.

The blockchain-based virtual reality platform Decentraland, which runs on Ethereum's blockchain, has already implemented this idea. As non-financial tokens (NFTs) grow more sophisticated and are linked into financial infrastructure, it may become feasible to apply the same idea of tokenized parcels of land, each with a different value and location, in the real world.

CHAPTER 11

NFTS for Gaming, Digital Identity, Licensing, Certificates and Fine Art

Non-fungible tokens have swept across the art world like wildfire. However, despite the fact that the technology has been available for many years, NFTs had their 'moment' earlier in 2021 when many high-profile artists made news by selling NFTs for millions of dollars each.

The NFT ownership paradigm, which does not need the possession of any physical items or intellectual property, represented a revolutionary shift in the way people thought about creative ownership. According to Monica Eaton-Cardone, Co-Founder and Chief Operating Officer of Chargebacks911, "in a sense, the conventional fine art industry has always been a manufactured bubble since we allocate value based on abstract advantages, such as prestige, rarity, and asceticism, rather than anything tangible."

Identity, Licensing, and Certification

Because non-fungible tokens are completely unique digital objects, non-fungible token applications in the context of digital identification have been identified.

The usage of NFTs may be used to "tokenize important papers," such as "identification cards, birth certificates, credentials and licenses, and other documents that can't be interchanged," according to Harriet Chan, Market Officer of software development company CocoFinder.

According to Ankit Bhatia, the CEO and Co-Founder of the Ethereum-based social network Sapien, in essence, "NFTs may serve as an irreversible record for achievement across settings, whether they are community-driven or focused on educational qualifications."

"I can fake a diploma or a certificate, but an NFT-based certification cannot be forged, particularly when the certification can be traced back to a source such as a university or an e-learning platform and the token is made non-transferable," he said.

Certifications of Authenticity and Ownership

Non-fungible tokens, in addition to being used for human identification and qualification certification, may be used to provide certifications of authenticity or ownership for any digital or physical item, regardless of its origin.

In an interview with Finance Magnates, Matt Zarracina, CEO of True Tickets, said that "many of the potential use cases of NFTs include unique asset ownership."

NFTs in the Gaming Industry

Continuing, Zarracina said that "other sectors where the scarcity and uniqueness of digital material generate value, such as gaming, are some of the biggest possibilities for NFTs in the short future." "Gaming and esports are two of the fastest-growing users of NFTs, with both industries relying on the technology to safeguard virtual assets earned while participating or playing."

According to a recent article from Finance Magnates, players have the opportunity to acquire unique accessories that may be used to enhance the appearance of their characters or the environments in which they live in a broad range of gaming ecosystems. In certain games, these digital goods may even be sold for real-world money, and in some cases, for substantial sums of money.

The ownership of digital goods was formerly tied to the platform on which the game was played: mistakes, hacks, or the discontinuance of a game could all be used to revoke the ownership of valuable digital items effectively. Digital ownership, on the other hand, may extend outside a particular game environment when using NFTs.

"With NFTs, players can sell virtual assets back and forth safely, while also taking their in-game money with them when they leave, a practice that is already being implemented in a number of games," Zarracina said.

Finance Magnates have reported that the usage of non-fungible tokens in gaming has the potential to generate whole virtual economies.

Even prior to the epidemic, she said, the video gaming business had already overtaken the motion picture industry, and she added that it hasn't come close to catching up. "The gaming community is enormous. 'The virtual world' of video games is just as absorbing as the'real world,' according to millions of Americans and many more people across the globe. The majority of them would rather spend their time and money on updating their avatars than on renovating their homes."

"NFTs provide you the opportunity to project status and uniqueness. In the future, as video games become more adept at blurring the boundaries between fiction and reality, the psychological attraction of nonfictional stories will almost certainly continue to increase. It's natural that gamers, who spend the majority of their spare time immersed in a hypnotically realistic, profoundly digital environment, would choose to spend their money on improving the living quarters of their virtual avatars instead of updating their own.

NFTs in Live Events and Experiences

Zarracina went on to say that NFT technology may be utilized for a variety of purposes other than gaming, including "linking back to or unlocking future unique experiences." For example, true Tickets, founded by Zarracina, specializes in blockchain-based ticketing for live entertainment venues.

"Through our work, which involves assisting live entertainment venues in transitioning to digital ticketing for all of their events, we have learned that customers mourn the loss of the physical ticket stub," he added.

After that, the issue is whether someone regrets the loss of their ticket stub or whether they mourn the loss of its capacity to elicit a particular memory or experience. In most cases, it's the latter, and NFTs are in a unique position to perform a comparable role, although digitally, and elicit these memories and emotions." To put it another way, NFT-based ticket stubs may function as digital collectibles in and of themselves.

He also said that "NFTs may play a role in unlocking future unique experiences," which is another benefit of the technology. To illustrate, a sports club might provide incentives to season ticket holders who attend every home game over the course of the season. Their presence would then provide them a one-of-a-kind NFT as well as access to a special experience that was only accessible to those who attended every home game."

As a result, NFTs are no longer a separate collectible, but rather are integrated into a broader experience between an organization and its supporters," the authors explain. The long-term potential of non-profit organizations to connect fans and customers in these ways is very intriguing."

Additionally, at the most fundamental level, NFTs may be utilized to improve the security of event tickets. According to Stefan von Imhof, the Co-Founder of the Alternative Assets Club, "counterfeit tickets are a significant problem, and since NFT ownership is traceable on a blockchain, the validity of an NFT ticket is always assured."

CHAPTER 12

Problems or Controversies Surrounding NFT

Legal issues surrounding NFTs:

The development, distribution, ownership, and trading of NFTs are all novel phenomena that pose a slew of legal problems, many of which are unclear or unresolved at the time of their emergence. In the next section, we will examine some of the most common legal concerns that should be considered by anybody engaged in the production, sale, or purchase of an NFT.

i.) Copyright

When you purchase an NFT, you are not purchasing the digital work in its whole. What you are purchasing is simply a collection of code known as metadata, which serves as a connection to the 'original' version of that work that you are purchasing. This metadata is put into the blockchain and includes information about where the original work is stored as well as who owns the specific version of the work that is being written into the blockchain. Anyone else is free to download and examine the digital artwork, and this does not prohibit them from doing so.

When you purchase an NFT, there is a widespread misunderstanding that you are also purchasing the rights to the digital artwork. This isn't the case at all. As a matter of fact, the situation is basically the same as if you were purchasing an artwork. When you purchase a painting, you are just purchasing the actual artwork itself; you are not purchasing the right to duplicate and sell copies of the painting or to create new works that are completely or substantially identical to the original. The same is true of non-financial transactions: no copyright is immediately obtained. Most NFT owners have no rights other than the ability to buy, sell, lend, or transfer their holdings of the NFT itself, which is dependent on the specific conditions of the market place where they made their purchase. Each marketplace, and even each particular product, may have its own set of conditions, which should always be carefully reviewed before a transaction is completed to ensure that the buyer understands precisely what they are buying.

When someone produces and sells an NFT of an active work in which they have no rights of ownership, either in the work itself or in the copyright in it, the situation becomes more complicated and complicated. For example, consider the case of a Twitter account called "Global Art Museum," which posted in March 2021 about selling non-financial-transfers (NFTs) of public domain works without notifying the institutions that held the artworks in question (this later turned out to be a publicity stunt). Despite the fact that such conduct is unequivocally unethical, it is not always criminal.

A work's copyright expires and it enters the public domain (which in the United Kingdom occurs 70 years after an artist's death), and there is nothing to prevent anybody from creating a copy (for example, by photographing the work) and then selling that copy as an original (whether as an NFT or otherwise). Indeed, for more than two decades, museums and galleries have been digitizing and licensing artworks, with the proceeds going to the museums and galleries that own the artworks (though is a topic not without controversy itself). However, the idea of a non-affiliated third party making money off such copies is a quite different situation. It may seem to be a bit too blatant an attack on the public domain to be deemed appropriate. It may also be in violation of the contractual terms and restrictions that many museums and galleries set.

The scenario in which a third-party opportunist targets a work that is not in the public domain but is nonetheless protected by copyright, such as a current digital work, and mints it as an NFT is perhaps even more difficult to understand. For all intents and purposes, this seems to be a clear-cut instance of copyright infringement – and it very well might be, if the act of minting and selling the NFT includes creating a duplicate of the underlying digital work. However, this is not the case. On the other hand, if it does not, there may be an argument that no infringement has happened since the NFT itself is just a cryptographic token that is connected to the digital asset, and therefore there is no infringement. That is not to suggest that such exploitation would not give rise to other possible legal claims, such as those based on fraud or passing off in certain cases. In either instance, the outcome would be highly reliant on the facts and on the claims made by the NFT's developer regarding the underlying work in question.

Another potential obstacle in this situation may be the artist's moral rights, which include the right to have his work credited to him as well as the right to object to his work being treated in a negative manner. Unfortunately, even in the conventional art market, there is very little case law in these areas, therefore it is impossible to predict how such issues would play out in the digital world at this point in time.

Given the many risks, a buyer would be well advised to perform thorough due diligence before making a purchase. In particular, it would be desirable to determine if the seller is the true author of the work, has solid ownership to it, and has acquired the consent of any third parties whose intellectual property is included in the digital work. In addition, any platform's terms and conditions should be carefully reviewed to ensure that what is really offered for purchase is apparent. Equally essential, it is always necessary to do due diligence to ensure that both the artist and the website on which the digital asset is housed are well-established. Even if the digital artwork itself is linked to the NFT, it is possible that it is housed on the servers of a third-party website and is not protected by the blockchain. Therefore, if the website were to cease operations for whatever reason, the NFT would be rendered useless and redundant as a consequence of the loss of its connection to the internet.

ii.) SMART contracts

The selling of NFTs is governed by smart contracts. These are digital contracts in which the terms of the agreement are encoded in code and embedded inside the purchase tokens, which are used to make purchases. SMART contracts are often designed to function automatically when a pre-defined set of circumstances is met, which is known as the trigger condition. According to the smart contract code, upon resale of the NFT, a royalty payment to the inventor may be sent automatically by way of the code. It is impossible to alter, remove, or edit the code since it is permanently created as a token on the blockchain and cannot be changed. When using SMART contracts, the degree of trust needed between contracting parties is reduced since the contractual obligations will be executed automatically when a trigger event occurs, such as the receipt of money.

A consequence of the fact that smart contracts fulfil their contractual duties on their own initiative is that, in principle, fewer legal disputes should occur over their terms and execution. However, there is almost no case law, legislation, or regulation specifically regarding SMART contracts in the United States. This increases the issue of whether or not SMART contracts are really legally enforceable contracts. As a result, the Legislation Commission issued a request for evidence on December 17, 2020, in order to inform its scoping investigation, which would examine the existing law as it relates to SMART contracts. Until the publication of this study later this year, the legal status of SMART contracts in the United Kingdom remains in doubt. In reality, however, there seems to be no reason why a SMART contract should not be legally enforceable, provided that the terms of the contract are sufficiently explicit, both parties want to be rightfully bound, and both parties have given enough thought. However, what may make matters more complicated is that SMART contracts will usually work in conjunction with the text-based conditions and terms of the relevant marketplace, which may make things more complicated. Consequently, if the two don't line up in any specific way, there is the possibility of misunderstanding and ambiguity.

iii.) Money laundering

There have been some questions raised about whether the exorbitant amounts of money that are being spent on the NFT market, combined with the widespread use of cryptocurrency, are being used to circumvent the increasingly stringent anti-money laundering regulations that are being implemented around the world. After all, it may be difficult to comprehend why collectors are willing to pay hundreds of thousands of dollars on what some would argue are basically digital signatures and other forms of digital media. The more cynical observers may also refer to the timing of the increase in popularity of NFTs, which has coincided with the introduction of anti-money laundering laws into the mainstream art market for the first time (at least in Europe). When speaking on an art podcast, David Hockney, for example, described non-profit organizations as the domain of "crooks and swindlers."

According to the EU's Fifth Anti-Money Laundering Directive (5AMLD), which took effect in the United Kingdom on 10 January 2020, all "Art Market Participants" (i.e. anyone who participates in the sale or purchase of works of art valued at more than €10,000) are subject to a slew of new obligations and requirements. A key requirement is the need to do Client Due Diligence (CDD) in advance of any transaction in order to verify a purchaser's identity and source of money before proceeding with the transaction.

Is noteworthy that non-financial institutions (NFTs) are not clearly covered under the UK's regulatory framework. This defines a "piece of art" in the 1994 Value Added Tax Act framework, which is out of date in the context of internet-based digital art and is thus unenforceable. Furthermore, there is no mention of NFTs or other digital art forms in the 5AMLD, and there is no specific advice on the topic in the British Art Market Federation's 2020 Guidance on Anti-Money Laundering for Art Market Participants (Guidelines on Anti-Money Laundering for Art Market Participants).

This seems to put NFTs in something of a regulatory limbo, which may enhance the likelihood that high-value NFT transactions may be utilized to evade anti-money laundering laws in the future. After all, since there is no tangible artwork to carry, they are simple to sell in a covert manner.

Furthermore, they are often linked to a decentralized currency, enabling a high degree of anonymity in transactional activities. Nonetheless, it is important to notice, that in the United Kingdom, criminals who use their ill-gotten profits to purchase NFTs as part of an effort to clean those money may still be accused under the Proceeds of Crime Act 2002.

After all, now that non-traditional works of art (NFTs) are unquestionably a part of the mainstream art market and their legitimacy is becoming more widely recognized, it appears only a matter of time before these digital artworks are brought under the purview of the United Kingdom's anti-money laundering regulations. If this were to occur, art market players in the digital art business would be required to register with HMRC, perform comprehensive CDD, and comply with other legal requirements, among other things. This would have a main impact on the character of NFT transactions and the market as a whole in the future.

iv.) Estate and succession planning

When it comes to digital collectibles, one issue that investors of these flourishing assets (particularly those belonging to Generation Z) may not have addressed is how the UK's legal system deals with these assets after the owner's death. Given the growing number of estates that now have a digital presence, this is becoming an increasingly significant issue. When it comes to assets such as NFTs, this has highlighted the need of comprehensive estate planning.

One of the most persistent apprehensions is how to deal with access to NFTs after a person's death, given that they (like crypto assets) can only be accessed with a unique personal key and password. As a result, stakeholders should at the very least take a few simple precautions to reduce the likelihood that these potentially lucrative assets will be lost for all time (and there are a terrifying number of well-known examples of private keys and passwords to digital assets being forgotten or misplaced).

Personal representatives are often made aware of these assets as a first step in the majority of instances (and to professional advisers). Preparing an inventory that includes information on the asset(s) and how to access them (as well as ensuring that it is updated on a regular basis and stored securely) will aid in the administration of the estate. As a result, it will be more probable that the individuals who the investor intended to gain from the assets (if any) would really benefit from them. Suppose non-financial assets (NFTs) are not included in an estate plan to be passed on to beneficiaries. In that case, there is a chance that they may be sold or liquidated, which may be contrary to the owner's wishes.

Due to the fact that a Will becomes accessible to the public after the award of probate, it is advised that sensitive information, such as instructions on how to access a testator's NFTs, be maintained in a separate document/memorandum that is held securely. This will aid in the development of a more comprehensive "digital legacy" strategy.

With the rise of NFTs and crypto assets, technology development in this area has unavoidably accelerated. As a result, not only is it now possible to back up these digital legacy plans using cloud data storage suppliers, but there are also sophisticated products in the industry that have been created specifically for these assets. In the context of crypto assets, for example,'multi-sig wallets' allow users to delegate a 'back-up key' to a third party in the event of a security breach. With this technology, personal representatives of the owner's estate are able to collect money on behalf of the owner's beneficiaries after the owner's death has taken place. For a variety of motives, including the rapid rate of development in NFT technology and the changing legal landscape in this sector, investors should be aware of the security risks presented by cyber-hacking.

While we have discussed how these assets may be handled upon death, we can anticipate a rise in the number of people who wish to include specific authority relating to digital assets in their estate planning documents, such as in a lasting power of attorney in the event of mental incapacity or in a living will.

Inheritance trusts: Inheritance trusts are often used as an estate planning tool to avoid the requirement for assets to go through the probate process. Though owning digital collectibles such as NFTs may seem to be appealing to investors (for a variety of reasons, including those related to secrecy), trustees must carefully examine their approach to investing and fulfilling their fiduciary obligations when it comes to holding NFTs. Because of the speculative and volatile character of these assets, trustees must be aware of any limitations on their investing abilities, such as their ability to diversify their portfolios, among other things. In addition, when trusts are used to hold such assets, attention should be made to adding extra provisions related to non-financial trusts (NFTs) in the trust documents (i.e. concerning liability, management or delegation).

v.) Taxation

Another area in which the law has not yet kept up with the rise in popularity of non-traditional financial institutions is the issue of taxes. NFTs are explicitly addressed in a paucity of law and advice, both in the United Kingdom and across the world. In the United Kingdom, the newly revised 'Crypto-assets Manual' of HMRC is primarily concerned with cryptocurrency. NFTs come into a somewhat distinct type of digital asset, and according to the handbook, NFTs are individually identifiable and thus are not 'pooled' for the purposes of Capital Gains Tax (CGT) calculations. It seems apparent that capital gains or losses on the sale of non-financial assets (NFTs) may be subject to CGT, and that they are almost certainly subject to Inheritance Tax and other UK taxes, but the exact tax situation is still unclear.

One especially challenging problem is identifying where non-financial corporations (NFTs) are located for taxation reasons. This is a critical problem for owners who have a foreign domicile and whose assets are located outside of the United Kingdom and thus are not subject to UK tax. HMRC's position on cryptocurrencies is that they are taxed in the jurisdiction where the beneficial owner resides, and they may adopt the same approach with NFTs, particularly if the underlying artwork is in digital form, but the law is ambiguous on this.

CHAPTER 13

Climate-Positive Crypto Art

When it comes to anything from selling illiquid assets such as real estate to combating counterfeiting, non-fungible tokens (NFTs) have been hailed as a panacea. A recent use case that has been pushed is digital art expressed as NFTs, which has the potential to combat climate change and create a more sustainable digital economy in the long run. Whether NFTs are a solution for many of the world's problems or another moment of collective lunacy driven by crypto collectors with more money than reason, the question is whether this era will be remembered as such.

NFTs As A Force for Good

The world is becoming digital, with virtual replacing physical, and nanostructured thin films (NFTs) have emerged as the answer to a diverse range of issues. If its creators are to be believed, NFTs have the potential to align incentives between artists and fans, provide verifiable scarcity, revolutionize e-gaming, and fuel a growing market for digital collectibles, among other things.

NFTs have been accused of worsening climate change, but do they have the ability to really help the cause of this global calamity?

According to the theory, since NFTs are produced and exchanged on energy-intensive blockchains that use enormous quantities of electricity, they are directly responsible for environmental damage. Furthermore, cryptocurrency blockchains, such as Ethereum (albeit less energy-intensive than bitcoin), are utilized for the smart contracts needed to mint and trade the NFTs, resulting in a direct carbon intensity connected with them that is climate-related in nature.

Not everyone believes that non-fossil-fuelled vehicles (NFTs) are responsible for the destruction of the environment. Some artists think that the polar opposite is true, while others disagree. The carbon footprint of NFTs has been greatly exaggerated, but when issued on low-energy blockchains, they may be a force for good, sustaining a flourishing market for digital art while also offsetting carbon usage and reducing greenhouse gas emissions in the process.

Beeple, SAF, and the Conscience Collective are all members of the Conscience Collective.

Even individuals who do not spend their time searching crypto chat groups for the newest 'NFT jewels' and must-have collectibles are likely to be familiar with Beeple's work. After his piece 'Everydays: The First 5000 Days' sold for a world-record $69.3 million at Christie's, the once-obscure digital artist is on his way to becoming a household brand. Consequently, Beeple ranked third among the most expensive living artists to have sold at auction, according to Artnet.

An even more ambitious NFT project is being planned by Beeple, in collaboration with digital artists such as Refik Anadol, Andres Resigner, Sara Ludy, and Kyle Gordon, who will all be participating. Several pieces of artwork contributed by the group of NFT artists will be sold via the Social Alpha Foundation (SAF), a blockchain-focused charitable organization. The Open Earth Foundation, a registered charity dedicated to cutting-edge research and implementation on the use of open digital infrastructure, such as blockchains, for climate accounting under the Paris Agreement, will receive hundred percent of the profits from the sale of the artwork. The #CarbonDrop auction is now trending on Twitter in the realm of NFT.

A carbon offset auction including 500 tonnes of carbon offsets that are also represented as one-of-a-kind NFTs has been made possible by the RNDR token, whose parent product, 'Octane,' drives most NFT visuals. As a consequence of the effort, carbon offsets have been recorded and are being used to support the preservation of the Amazon rainforest and the prevention of deforestation. It's tough to find fault with the motivation behind the environmental fundraiser. However, is it possible for such efforts to make a significant contribution to the fight against climate change? Or, alternatively, might the answer to the NFT blockchain Ethereum's energy usage be found somewhere else - such as on another blockchain?

We have found it to be very inspirational to collaborate with these incredible artists in order to raise climate awareness and money for vital digital public goods." For the mainstream environmental space, our work on global climate technology tends to be very innovative; however, our work on global climate technology is not particularly innovative for artists who are pushing the boundaries of their respective fields with technology," says Martin Wainstein, founder and executive director of Open Earth Foundation.

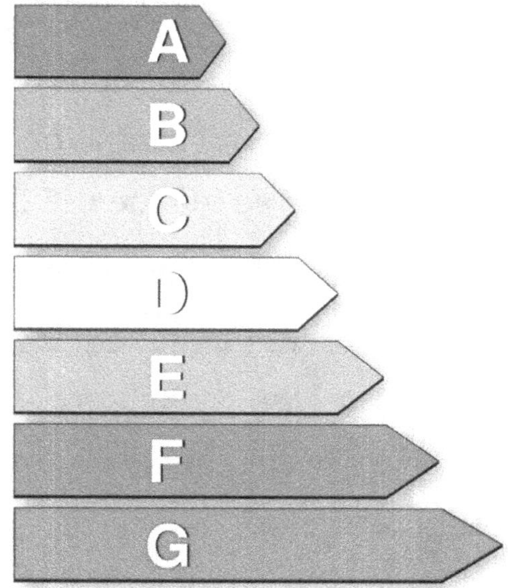

Putting Your Money Into a Low-Energy Future

It is no coincidence that Bitcoin and Ethereum are the world's most energy-intensive blockchains. This is a result of the revenue model, which requires miners to link power-hungry ASICs and crunch numbers in a race to discover new blocks and collect rewards. Thus, it would be dishonest to claim that Proof of Work blockchains are beneficial to the environment, despite the fact that most of the energy required to mine bitcoin comes from renewable sources. And no amount of money collected by carbon sequestration fundraisers will be able to make up for this.

There may be alternative networks that may help solve the energy issue that blockchain is experiencing – particularly the one ascribed to NFTs. The vast majority of blockchains that have popped up since Ethereum have used Proof of Stake, a low-energy method of protecting blockchains in which validators lock – or stake – assets into a smart contract as an incentive behave in accordance with ethical standards. As long as validators adhere to the network's consensus rules, they will be rewarded with tokens, much as miners who protect Proof of Work chains are paid.

Ethereum itself is in the process of moving from Proof of Work to Proof of Stake, but the change is complicated and time-consuming. Meanwhile, miners continue to crunch billions of calculations every second to protect the Ethereum network, which is secured via the use of Proof of Work.

To persuade users of cryptocurrency to move to low-energy alternatives was always going to be a difficult sell. On the other hand, users now have a more concrete motivation to make the switch to Proof of Stake blockchains: money. To put it another way, Ethereum is too costly to use. According to the Energy Information Administration, demand for block space, driven by DeFi and NFTs, has pushed gas prices to all-time highs. The fact that retail users are being priced out of performing onchain transactions, which regularly exceed $100 per transaction, is causing Proof of Stake networks that were previously inactive or under construction to acquire momentum.

The most notable of them is Polygon (previously Matic), a low-cost and scalable blockchain that links to the Ethereum blockchain. Polygon's ecosystem of decentralized apps (dApps) has proved to be a fruitful breeding ground for new financial technologies (NFTs), which are flourishing in the low-energy, low-fee environment provided by Polygon. Numerous NFT-focused initiatives, including a number constructing inside Decentraland's metaverse (a user-owned virtual environment), have set up business on Polygon, including a number building within the Decentraland metaverse. TradeStars, Battle Racers, and Decentral Games are examples of such companies, with the latter developing virtual casinos that can be visited from inside Decentraland.

Because of the attention being focused on Ethereum's energy cost, Tezos is another smart contract chain that is benefitting from the attention being focused on Ethereum's energy bill. In addition, AI artist Mike Tyka has chosen Tezos as the platform for launching his NFT collection, citing the

Proof of Stake blockchain's environmental credentials as the reason for his decision.

With a single click of a button, Tyka, who has a PhD in biophysics and is aware of the need to promote sustainability, said that "minting NFTs using Ethereum would wipe away years of attempting to minimise my own climate impact with the press of a mouse." Following my research and discovery of some suggested alternatives, I determined that if I was going to join this area, I should support what I believe to be the only viable and ethical future for NFTs.

The digital artist has also indicated a wish to use additional non-financial-transaction (NFT) markets that are based on PoS networks.

It is possible that the energy issue with NFTs may be resolved when projects seeking shelter from Ethereum's exorbitant fees migrate to Proof of Stake networks like as Polygon and Tezos, and as users follow in their footsteps. Digital collectors are only too ready to trade the newest NFTs, but they are wary of spending hundreds of dollars in fees for the pleasure of transacting with them. Instead, they can get the best of both worlds by participating in Proof of Stake chains: cheap costs while also receiving a pass on being involved in climate change.

Using New Technology to Solve Old Problems

The notion of blockchain technology enabling environmental benefits may appear fantastical, if not absurd at first glance. For one thing, the Paris Climate Agreement and its roadmap to net-zero emissions are managed through the global stocktake (GST), which will be held every five years starting in 2023; and the Agreement itself is completely separate from the contributions made by non-state actors such as corporations and subnational governments.

With the GST, the Open Earth Foundation hopes to supplement the government's efforts by enabling concerned people to address an old issue via the use of modern technologies such as NFTs. Consequently, rich art collectors and celebrities may participate in the hot new art NFT trend while simultaneously helping to carbon reduction and transparency in the global environment.

It goes without saying that self-awareness is essential for comprehending the daily activities that contribute to climate change. In order to do this, a month-long awareness campaign will be launched to encourage NFT and cryptocurrency stakeholders to mitigate their climate effect in any manner they can. The Open Earth Foundation will take part in the #carbondrop campaign, which will climax on April 22nd, which is Earth Day, in a fitting conclusion.

According to Beeple, his work will be carbon neutral or negative going forward. However, as environmental activists increase their pressure on the NFT industry, other NFT platforms, artists, and even purchasers will probably follow his lead. There are many possibilities here, including carbon offsetting, a commitment to more energy-efficient blockchains, financial incentives for artists whose work is carbon-neutral, and the list is endless.

NFTs are still in their infancy — despite the hoopla, they account for a relatively tiny proportion of total Ethereum transactions. Nevertheless, it is heartening to see that attempts are already being made to implement environmentally friendly methods, especially given the market's immaturity at this point. Is it possible that sensitive artists have had a role in this, or is the broad attention sparked by the NFT boom putting a light on the long-standing issue of blockchain energy consumption?

CHAPTER 14

Downsides of NFTS and Cryptocurrency

While non-profit organizations (NFTs) may open many new doors for artists, there are also drawbacks and dangers that you should be aware of.

Ownership and copyright are important concepts to understand.

Art theft is becoming more prevalent among NFTs. Stories have arisen in recent months of artists finding their work on internet markets, where it is being marketed as non-functional toys (NFTs) without their knowledge or permission.

This is because the framework on which NFTs function was created many years ago and has not been updated to reflect the manner in which internet users may sell and exchange decentralized assets, such as art.

A very early version of NFTs was packaged together in a 2017 "game" called CryptoKittties, which was based on the concept of quantum computing. A limited number of virtual cats (sold as NFTs) were available for purchase, and users were able to breed them with other players in the game. However, because these NFTs were developed by the game's creators at the time, they were only available in that particular gaming environment.

Due to the fact that the creators held the exclusive rights to the cats that could be purchased or sold, a player could not just upload a duplicate of a cat to sell or utilize to their advantage. Because the creators had complete control over who could and couldn't create new cats, they also had complete control over the quantity of cats available in the marketplace at any one moment. The cat market was not going to swell as a result of this.

But when it comes to the art industry, the producers of NFTs (in this instance, digital artists) have very little influence over how and where their work is shown and sold. As Wellington-based artist Pepper Raccoon argues, this was an issue long before NFTs came into the scene, and the dream that NFTs are attempting to offer artists is not what it seems to be on the surface.

"I do not believe that NFTs are effective in solving any of the issues that they claim to be effective in solving. In the end, it's all about selling optimism." As previously stated, the value proposition of NFTs is that the proof of work guarantees that your original item has a unique token associated with it, which means that the person who owns it knows they are in possession of a "original." However, the issue is that someone may take a JPG and post it on a separate marketplace, with a different token linked to it, and then sell it for profit. "There is no such thing as a 'original.'"

So, who has the authority to "mint" an NFT and who does not? The solution is straightforward: the artist should have ultimate control over the minting of their work (i.e., how many "original" copies are sold) as well as the locations where their work is available for purchase. However, because of the anarchy of the internet, putting that concept into action is challenging.

When you consider the financial difficulties that many artists have experienced in the past year, it's no surprise that the idea of selling work online is so alluring. It's easy to see why some artists have resorted to selling their work as non-financial tokens (NFTs) in order to make ends meet when you combine that with the new, hyped world of cryptocurrencies. As a result, artists should do some research into platforms that actively promote original work and select the sold items to prevent their work being possibly ripped off by others.

"There are other avenues [for selling digital art]," Raccoon explains. "Art Grab is a very amazing site that debuted lately and accepts fiat money as its payment method. You may license a picture, and it will be removed from the internet, and you will become the owner of the image. It's simply normal money that's being used.

The way it's set up, it's really a celebration of the artist, rather than just putting up a million dollars' worth of stuff. When I look at it, I see it as very curated, and I believe that has a lot to do with how value is fixed. Instead of saying, 'here's a marketplace with eight million anonymized tokens that you can purchase', it says, "These are artists that we believe in, these artists who are doing interesting things and pushing the boundaries," rather than "here's an anonymous token market where you can purchase."

Environment

In the same way that the NFT mechanism is obsolete, the Ethereum blockchain, on which NFTs are built, is also out of date, unable to keep up with the volume and scale of worldwide, frenzied adoption.

The Ether (cryptocurrency) that resides on the Ethereum blockchain, like its rival Bitcoin, may be "mined" (or "produced") by ordinary individuals using computers that solve difficult mathematical problems. These individuals get coins as a thank you for their efforts in mining the currency. And more the value of the coins rises, the greater the incentive for others to start mining becomes. It's basically a symbiotic relationship: if you scratch my back, I'll scratch yours, and vice versa,

The issue is that the amount of energy required to mine Bitcoin and Ethereum is enormous. Consider this: the energy needed to mine new Bitcoin generates more carbon dioxide emissions than the whole country of Aotearoa, to put it in context. According to some estimates, Bitcoin is on pace to surpass the entire energy usage of the city of London.

"A single piece of artwork sold as a non-financial transaction consumes at a least the equivalent of two weeks' worth of home energy in a single transaction," explains Raccoon. "

An increasing number of NFT markets are contemplating moving from a "proof of work" system (in which computers must solve certain equations in order to generate new coins) to a "proof of stake" one (in which coins are created by placing bets on the outcome of the game) (in which users must demonstrate ownership of their coin in order to produce new coins). As a result, provable stake systems (also known as proof of stake systems) are becoming more common.

In other words, users may effectively demonstrate that they own a part of the 'land' (or blockchain), thus increasing the perceived value of the asset and allowing for the production of new blocks to generate more value.

Will this systematic change have a positive influence on the climate-changing effects of blockchain technology? Perhaps just for a short while. However, the carbon emissions associated with Ethereum and Bitcoin mining are increasing at an alarming pace, necessitating a significant amount of innovation to resolve the issue completely. That type of innovation is expensive in terms of both money and time, and for the time being, the short-term financial benefits exceed the long-term environmental consequences for those who are engaged.

However, the environmental consequences of ethereum mining have prompted some artists to abandon their NFT efforts entirely until better environmentally friendly techniques can be used.

Barriers to entry and flow of money

Many wealthy and influential individuals from all around the world have invested in Ethereum, and as a result, they have a strong interest in seeing the cryptocurrency thrive. According to Raccoon, the same investors are the ones that pay the large checks that have made news in the past. According to the author, "the larger art purchases that you see taking place, like as the $69 million purchase of Beeple's artwork, were made by someone who has a vested interest in the development of cryptocurrencies."

Because of the 'pyramid' nature of the NFT system, it is very difficult for new artists to break through to the top rung. Many artists find it difficult to market their work because they lack a following or celebrity. According to Raccoon, "the individuals at the top of the food chain who are already renowned, those artists who are releasing NFTs and already have a big following are the ones who are earning money." "A lot of individuals are sold on the idea of earning thousands and thousands of dollars when, in fact, it's simply another more concentrated conventional art market," says the author of the book.

So what should artists do?

Raccoon is unafraid to express her point of view.

"Wait and see," she advises, adding that "the concept of imagined worth should be treated with caution." Whenever you're sold on the notion that your labour has fictitious worth – or virtual value on the internet - someone stands to profit from your efforts. It's critical to consider where the money is really going, which is why I believe that waiting is the best course of action."

The NFT market is still in its early stage, and, like many other immature markets, it is experiencing some teething issues and raising some significant concerns about its future. Is it going to crash and burn? Or will it evolve and become a more controlled platform, thus reducing the danger of copyright infringement and the power structures that now exist in the industry? Will new, more energy-efficient platforms develop to address some of the most energy-intensive elements of technology in the future?

Only time will be able to provide the answers to these questions. Although there has been debate about the unsustainable and unethical aspects of non-profit organizations (NFTs), the bottom line is that artists should be able to earn a living from their work without having to worry about contributing to a pyramid scheme, the demise of the Earth's ecology, or even the judgment of their peers.

And, if anything, the NFT market has sparked an important debate about how artists may earn money from the sale of their work in a society that is becoming more decentralized.

According to Raccoon, the notion of investing in a 'get-rich-quick' plan that damages the environment is immoral and harmful. "Artists should act with honesty and purpose," he adds. Even the effect of selling non-traditional works of art (NFTs) is significant: there is a significant portion of the art audience that is so terribly put off by this that you will lose part of your audience, and artists must determine if it is really worth it."

When considering the reaction against artists who choose to use non-traditional means of earning a living, it's essential to remember that such artists are not the source of the issue.

In spite of the fact that it may be easy to criticize or get angry at other artists for their participation in NFTs, adds Raccoon, "we need to be a community at the end of the day, and artists need to promote sustainable methods of earning a livelihood." "[The artists] are not the ones who are causing the problem; rather, it is the way that Ethereum is built, as well as the individuals who are benefiting from Ethereum, who are the ones who are causing the problem."

The Real Downsides of Cryptocurrency

An inordinate quantity of time has been spent extolling the virtues of blockchain technology and cryptocurrencies over the course of this series. In contrast, the negative aspects of cryptocurrencies have led some (such as well-known investor Warrant Buffet) to label them as the next "bubble" in the financial markets. Identifying and comprehending the drawbacks and obstacles that may impede broad adoption of these technologies is important in this respect. In particular,

Drawback #1: Scalability

The difficulties associated with scalability that cryptocurrencies provide are perhaps the most serious of the issues. However, although the number of digital currencies and their acceptance are growing quickly, they are still dwarfed by the number of transactions that the payment behemoth VISA conducts on a daily basis. Moreover, the speed of a transaction is another key measure with which cryptocurrencies will be unable to contend on an equal footing with companies such as VISA and Mastercard until the infrastructure that supports these technologies is substantially scaled up. Such a progress is complicated, and it is tough to complete in a smooth manner. However, others have already suggested a number of solutions to the scalability problem, including lightning networks, sharding, and staking, as well as other alternatives to consider.

Drawback #2: Cybersecurity issues

Because cryptocurrencies are a digital technology, they will be vulnerable to cybersecurity breaches and may fall into the hands of cybercriminals. We've already seen proof of this, with several initial coin offerings (ICOs) being hacked and investors losing hundreds of millions of dollars only this summer (one of these assaults alone resulted in a loss of $473 million to investors). Of course, mitigating this will need the ongoing maintenance of security infrastructure, but we are already seeing many players dealing with it directly and implementing improved cybersecurity measures that go above and beyond those employed in conventional banking sectors.

Price volatility and a lack of intrinsic value are the third and final disadvantages.

In the cryptocurrency ecosystem, price volatility, which is linked to a lack of intrinsic value, is a significant issue, and it is one of the details that Buffet alluded to explicitly a few weeks ago when he described the ecosystem as being in a bubble. It is a legitimate worry, but one that may be alleviated by explicitly connecting the value of bitcoin to physical and intangible goods (as we have seen some new players do with diamonds or energy derivatives). In addition, consumer confidence should rise due to increased adoption, which should help reduce volatility.

Drawback #2: Cybersecurity issues

During his speech, buffet also addressed this issue, saying, "It doesn't make any sense." There are no regulations in place for this. It's out of hand and out of control. No central bank, not even the United States Federal Reserve, or any other central bank, has jurisdiction over it. I have absolutely no faith in this whole endeavour. "I believe it's going to come crashing down."

Suppose we perfect the technology and eliminate all the issues mentioned above. In that case, there will still be greater risk associated with investing in this technology until it is accepted and controlled by the federal government.

The popular of the other issues about the technology are logistical in nature. A simple example is that altering procedures, which becomes required as technology advances, may take a long time and cause a halt in the regular flow of business activities.

The main takeaway is as follows:

With all of the potential obstacles to broad adoption, it is natural that seasoned professionals would be skeptical investors such as Warren Buffet would want to play it safe when it comes to this technology. Despite this, we are certain that cryptocurrencies (as well as blockchain technology) will be around for a long time. This is because they provide far too many of the benefits that customers are looking for in a currency today; decentralization, transparency, and flexibility are just a few of the advantages they provide. Extending the discussion to encompass all that blockchain technology is capable of across a broad variety of industries strengthens this point even more.

CHAPTER 15

The Next Big Thing in NFTs

NFTs are a tokenized form of assets (such as a tweet, art, music, and so forth) that can be exchanged on the blockchain, the public digital ledger technology that underpins cryptocurrencies, and other decentralized applications (such as Ethereum, Bitcoin, and Dogecoin). As soon as individuals who want to sell their work register with the marketplace and emboss digital tokens by uploading and verifying their information to the blockchain, these digital assets are transformed into NFTs. They then offer their works for auction on non-traditional markets (NFTs), which are analogous to eBay. When an NFT is bought, it is assigned a unique code that serves as evidence of ownership.

Having gained a basic understanding of what an NFT is, you may find yourself with more questions than answers. Don't be concerned; we've got you covered.

What Is the Distinction Between Cryptocurrency and Non-Fiat Treaties?

You may have noticed that individuals who have invested in cryptocurrencies have most likely also invested in non-financial tokens (NFTs). Unfortunately, NFTs and cryptocurrencies are not the same thing, despite being both created using comparable code and seem to attract the same audience.

The most significant distinction is the degree to which they are fungible. Cryptocurrency, like the paper dollar, has the property of being fungible. This implies that one Bitcoin can be traded for another Bitcoin in the same way that a dollar bill can be interchanged for another dollar bill.

In contrast to cryptocurrencies, the National Futures Trust cannot be exchanged or resold into the market. Because the underlying asset is unique and has a digital signature, each NFT is unique and cannot be traded for a fixed amount of money with another NFT of the same value. Instead, NFTs are often seen as an investment in art, with the expectation that the value of the investment would increase with time.

The fact that Ethereum is a prominent cryptocurrency as well as being a kind of blockchain technology should not be overlooked. The cryptocurrency exchanges their coins based on their blockchain technology; however, you cannot buy the blockchain itself through the cryptocurrency exchange. Furthermore, because Ethereum's blockchain allows non-volatile memory tokens (NFTs) to store extra information, the technology is distinct from the Ethereum currencies.

What is it about NFTs that makes them so popular?

This may come as a surprise to learn that NFTs were first introduced in 2015. Following the sale of a single collectible from the Cryptopunk series for more than $1 million in February, NFTs have gained national attention and have become a popular trending topic on Twitter.

What exactly was the valuable collectible item that was worth so much cash? Pixel art is a kind of art that uses pixels to create a picture.

While the bulk of the public was taken aback by the fact that a piece of digital art might be worth millions of dollars, other artists jumped on the bandwagon and attempted to create works worth millions of dollars of their own.

As a result, there has been a boom in the digital art industry, particularly in the market for non-fungible tokens. NFTs have continued to create news as a result of their ability to change hands at astronomical prices. In an unprecedented instance of digital art, a real artwork produced by the humanoid robot Sophia and sold as an NFT for about $700,000 has been sold for approximately $700,000.

Although the NFT market is appealing to both buyers and sellers, it is particularly appealing to the artists themselves. In the minds of many digital artists, the future is one in which NFT changes their creative process as well as how the public perceives "useful art." Using this internet market, artists may connect with potential customers without the necessity to exhibit their work in a gallery setting.

What Is the Future of Non-Ferrous Metals?

Realistically, a decline in NFT pricing is unavoidable, as a massive flood of new NFTs enters the markets, many of which were manufactured by individuals expecting to profit from the present trend.

More and more celebrities are beginning to offer their own non-alcoholic beverages. Sales of works by artists such as Grimes (Claire Elise Boucher) and Twitter founder and CEO Jack Dorsey are in the millions, while other producers have not been so fortunate. Some individuals are concerned that as more celebrities and influencers join the market, the work of the ordinary local artist will become much less valuable as a result.

Even if the market for digital art NFTs begins to decline, this does not imply the collapse of the NFT industry as a whole. On the contrary, every day, it seems, a new participant enters the market, broadening the concept of what a non-financial transaction (NFT) is and what it may become.

NFTs have just recently entered the gaming sector, yet they are already causing havoc in the industry. Traditionally, you purchase things to use in the game, and after you have finished with them, they are of no additional use to you. Instead, the digital assets for auction in a game are owned by the game's developers, and the players who purchase these things will resell them once they have finished the game. The conventional approach is completely altered as a result of this. In-game purchases will now be seen as investments rather than as a one-time expenditure of a few hundred dollars.

As the market for NFTs expands, we will witness a resurgence and a decline in some patterns. For example, because digital art is so easily accessible, it is underappreciated to a significant extent. On the other hand, some believe that the development and acceptance of NFTs are propelling us toward a Blockchain revolution that will fundamentally alter consumer capitalism as we now know it.

Which non-financial technologies (NFTs) should you invest in?

If you are considering investing in non-financial technologies, there is a lot to understand. An NFT is only worth what someone is willing to pay for it, which is the current market value. The number of recommendations and criteria to follow when monitoring whether meme or tweet is a smart investment is quite limited. Because of the unpredictability and the fact that NFTs are relatively new, it is difficult to predict how much your one-of-a-kind piece of digital art will be valued in the future.

People that want to take risks with their investments may wish to take advantage of the potential that NFTs may provide, while more conservative investors may want to be more cautious with their money. Due to the fact that we are not financial advisers and do not provide investment advice, we commend that you contact your financial advisor for investment advice tailored to your specific financial circumstances.

Was there anything else Blockchain Technology was capable of?

In its Blockchain-Based Transformation Trend Insight Report, Gartner states that most company executives are turning to blockchain mainly to improve existing processes and records management; nevertheless, digital assets and decentralization may now also benefit from blockchain adoption.

Gartner forecasts that these advantages will be achieved in the future, but that this will take time. According to a report, only 10% of enterprises will experience any significant transformation as a result of blockchain technology by 2022; by 2026, however, It is predicted that blockchain technology would be worth more than $360 billion by 2020, with the value of blockchain technology increasing to an estimated $3.1 trillion by 2030. Not even a shaky-digital-stick-shaking gesture is appropriate here!

Conclusion

Because of the rapid growth and popularity of NFTs and the Cryptoart industry, new and alternative routes and choices are developing that provide a far more ecologically friendly approach to the Ethereum blockchain and other distributed ledger technologies.

Perhaps the best answer is not to totally invalidate this market, but rather to investigate other options that will allow the growth of NFTs and Cryptoart in an environmentally and socially responsible manner. The development of these new platforms is accelerating, but the issue is that they do not yet have the volume or equivalent of Bitcoin or Ethereum platforms, which are the industry leaders.

It is the ability to build a blockchain without the requirement for a mining farm or proof of work that these new platforms are giving its users. A range of blockchains that operate in an ecologically sustainable manner are used by the new platforms, including PoS, PoA, and many others. You can discover a variety of blockchains that operate in an environmentally sustainable manner here.

As a consequence, implementing these blockchains would be a thousand times more efficient, allowing for a reduction in CO_2 emissions. As a result, there should be sufficient demand for these greener, more environmentally friendly platforms and transparent platforms to spur the development of new developers, investors, and collectors to invest in and develop these greener, more environmentally friendly platforms, thereby expanding the marketplace.

Non-financial transactions (NFTs) are establishing a new market for artists and collectors to sell their "signature" digital goods in a way that makes unsigned versions of the materials accessible to the general public. The parties involved in the sale or acquisition of NFTs should make certain that they understand the consequences of the transaction for copyright rights. In addition, any member of the public wishing to make any substantial use of an NFT picture (e.g., sell, distribute, or preserve copies) should obtain competent legal counsel to ensure that any problems of copyright are handled.